THE GREAT WHITE FLEET

THE GREAT WHITE FLEET

TONY RANTZ

ABOOKS
Alive Book Publishing

The Great White Fleet
Copyright © 2024 by Anthony L. Rantz

All rights reserved. No part of this book may be reproduced or transmitted in any form or by any means without written permission from the publisher and author.

Additional copies may be ordered from the publisher for educational, business, promotional or premium use. For information, contact ALIVE Book Publishing at: alivebookpublishing.com, or call (925) 837-7303.

Book Design by Alex P. Johnson
Cover Photo: Library of Congress

ISBN 13
978-1-63132-232-7

Library of Congress Control Number: 2024909315
Library of Congress Cataloging-in-Publication Data is available upon request.

First Edition

Published in the United States of America by ALIVE Book Publishing
an imprint of Advanced Publishing LLC
3200 A Danville Blvd., Suite 204, Alamo, California 94507
alivebookpublishing.com

PRINTED IN THE UNITED STATES OF AMERICA

10 9 8 7 6 5 4 3 2 1

Dedicated to

Carolyn Symes, David Rantz, and Michael Rantz

Introduction

The "Great White Fleet" sent around the world by President Theodore Roosevelt from 16 December 1907 to 22 February 1909 consisted of sixteen new battleships of the Atlantic Fleet. The battleships were painted white except for gilded scrollwork on their bows. The Atlantic Fleet battleships only later came to be known as the "Great White Fleet."

The fourteen-month long voyage was a grand pageant of American sea power. The squadrons were manned by 14,000 sailors. They covered some 43,000 miles and made twenty port calls on six continents.

The battleships were accompanied during the first leg of their voyage by a "Torpedo Flotilla" of six early destroyers, as well as by several auxiliary ships. The destroyers and their tender did not actually steam in company with the battleships, but followed their own itinerary from Hampton Roads to San Francisco. Two battleships were detached from the fleet at San Francisco, and two others substituted.

With the USS *Connecticut* as flagship under the command of Rear Admiral Robley D. Evans, the fleet sailed from Hampton Roads, Virginia, on 16 December 1907 for Trinidad, British West Indies, thence to Rio de Janeiro, Brazil; Sandy Point, Chile; Callao, Peru; Magdalena Bay, Mexico, and up the west coast, arriving at San Francisco, 6 May 1908.

After the arrival of the fleet off the west coast, the USS *Glacier* was detached and later became the supply ship of the Pacific Fleet. At this time also, the USS *Nebraska*, Captain Reginald F. Nicholson, and the USS *Wisconsin*, Captain Frank E. Beatty, were substituted for the USS *Maine* and USS *Alabama*.

At San Francisco, Rear Admiral Charles S. Sperry assumed command of the Fleet, owing to the poor health of Admiral Evans. Leaving that port on 7 July, 1908, the U.S. Atlantic Fleet visited Honolulu, Hawaii; Auckland, New Zealand; Sydney, Melbourne and Albany, Australia; Manila, Philippine Islands; Yokohama, Japan; Colombo, Ceylon; arriving at Suez, Egypt, on 3 January 1909.

In Egypt, word was received of an earthquake in Sicily, thus affording an opportunity for the United States to show it's friendship to Italy by offering aid to the sufferers. The *Connecticut*, *Illinois*, *Culgoa* and *Yankton* were dispatched to Messina at once. The crew of the *Illinois* recovered the bodies of the American consul and his wife, entombed in the ruins.

The *Scorpion*, the Fleet's station ship at Constantinople, and the *Celtic*, a refrigerator ship fitted out in New York, were hurried to Messina, relieving the *Connecticut* and *Illinois*, so that they could continue on the cruise.

Leaving Messina on 9 January 1909, the Fleet stopped at Naples, Italy, thence to Gibraltar, arriving at Hampton Roads, Virginia, on 22 February 1909. There President Roosevelt reviewed the Fleet as it passed into the roadstead.

Book One

SOUVENIR....

Official Reception and Luncheon

TENDERED BY

The City of Philadelphia

TO

3d Pennsylvania Volunteer Infantry

ON ITS RETURN FROM

SPANISH-AMERICAN WAR,

Industrial Hall,   ❧ ❧ ❧   September 10, 1898.

1879–1898.

3d Pennsylvania Volunteer Infantry

Menu

CHICKEN CROQUETTES WITH PEAS

CHICKEN SALAD

FRIED OYSTERS

CRAB SALAD   POTATO SALAD

COLD HAM   COLD TONGUE

SWISS CHEESE

SLICED TOMATOES

PICKLES   COLD SLAW

COFFEE

VIENNA ROLLS   BREAD AND BUTTER

GINGER ALE   APOLLINARIS

BEER

City Committee

Hon. CHARLES F. WARWICK, Chairman

Gen. Geo. R. Snowden,
Col. Robt. B. Beath,
Gen. H. S. Huidekoper,
Gen. Edw. Morrell,
Col. R. Dale Benson,
Col. A. Loudon Snowden,
Gen. Louis Wagner,
Gen. St. Clair A Mulholland,
Col. T. E. Wiedersheim,
Col. S. Bonnaffon, Jr.,
Col. Alex. P. Colesberry,
Col. William W Allen,
Major W Wesley Chew,
Capt. W. S. Poulterer,
Capt. Chas J. Hendler,
Capt. J. Campbell Gilmore,
Lieut W Howard Pancoast,
Dr. Wilmer R Batt,
Dr. M S. French,
Rev H. L. Duhring,

Col. Geo. F. Leland,
Col. O. C. Bosbyshell,
C. Stuart Patterson,
Justus C. Strawbridge,
John H. Converse,
Wm. J. Latta,
Capt. R P Schellenger,
Jacob J. Seeds,
James L. Miles,
Wencil Hartman,
Louis S. Amonson
Edward W. Patton,
Wm. Van Osten,
Geo. D McCreary,
Joshua L. Bailey
A. H. Ladner, Esq.,
C. Fotteral McMichael,
S Murdock Kendrick
Theo. W. Reath,
Capt. Thos J. Powers.

George W Edmonds.

BOOK TWO

THE Washington Monthly

"National Patriotism is the Strength of the Nation"

United States Ship Washington.

MAGDALENA BAY, MEXICO.

Vol. 1.   February, 1908.   No. 3.

THE WASHINGTON MONTHLY.

Printed and Published on board the
U. S. S. WASHINGTON.

Vol. 1. February, 1908. No. 3.

ITINERARY OF CRUISE.

Ports visited.	Arrived.	Left.	Miles.
League Island, Pa. (Commissioned)	Aug 7-06	Nov 1-06	
Newport News, Va.	Nov 2-06	" 6-06	165
Hampton Roads, Va.	" 6-06	" 8-06	8
Piney Point, Va.	" 8-06	" 8-06	97
Colon, Panama.	" 14-06	" 15-06	1839
Chirique Lagoon, Panama.	" 16-06	" 18-06	131
Mona Passage.	" 21-06	" 22-06	1000
Newport News, Va.	" 26-06	Dec 8-06	1220
League Island, Pa.	Dec 11-06	Apr 11-07	261
Hampton Roads, Va.	Apr 12-07	" 14-07	154
Lynnhaven Bay, Va.	" 14-07	" 16-07	18
Hampton Roads, Va.	" 16-07	May 9-07	17
Sandy Hook Light Ship.	May 10-07	" 10-07	241
Navy Yard, New York.	" 10-07	" 28-07	31
Tompkinsville, N. Y.	" 28-07	Jun 5-07	8
Hampton Roads, Va.	Jun 6-07	" 11-07	266
Bradford, R. I.	" 12-07	" 13-07	381
Newport, R. I.	" 13-07	" 14-07	8
Royan, France.	" 23-07	Jul 2-07	3128
Ile D' Aix, France.	Jul 2-07	" 3-07	37
La Pallice, France.	" 3-07	" 11-07	14
Brest, France.	" 12-07	" 25-07	234
Tompkinsville, N. Y.	Aug 6-07	Aug 17-07	3252
Newport, R. I.	" 18-07	" 21-07	165
Tompkinsville, N. Y.	" 24-07	" 24-07	542 ✦
Navy Yard, New York.	" 24-07	Oct 1-07	8
Hampton Roads, Va.	Oct 2-07	" 12-07	276
Port of Spain, Trinidad, B. W. I.	" 18-07	" 24-07	1799
Rio de Janeiro, Brazil.	Nov 4-07	Nov 10-07	3301
Montevideo, Uruguay.	,, 13-07	,, 19-07	1036
Punta Arenas, Chile.	,, 23-07	,, 27-07	1321
Callao, Peru.	Dec 5-07	Dec 12-07	2788
Acapulco, Mexico.	,, 19-07	,, 22-07	2179
Pichilinque Bay, Mexico.	,, 25-07	,, 28-07	775
Magdalena Bay, Mexico.	,, 29-07	----	312

(Had trial trip on this run; average speed 21.8 knots for four hour run) ✦

"Our Cruise"
(Continued from last issue)

While at Callao no shore leave was granted the crew owing to the fact that an epidemic of small pox was reported to exist in the city of Lima, with cases of Bubonic plague in both Lima and Callao. Only a few men were allowed ashore on duty.

Callao, which extends for about two miles along the beach that fronts the bay, has a population of about 50,000. Though always spoken of as the port of Lima, the capital of Peru, it is fast becoming an important city on its own account, and it may be said to enjoy uninterrupted fine weather at all seasons of the year.

There is nothing of interest to be seen at Callao, and one is quite ready to hasten to the capital which is ten miles distant, and is connected with Callao by an excellent electric car system.

For a city only about 700 miles south of the equator, Lima has the most remarkable climate in the world, never uncomfortably warm, nearly always cloudy with never a drop of rain. The soil is very fertile and everything is grown entirely by irrigation. With tropical rainfall it would be one of the most fertile tropical places in the world, but the city of Lima would disappear, for the buildings are made principally of adobe (sun-baked mud and bricks), and with a heavy rainfall these adobe buildings would melt away.

Overcoming our northern prejudice against the sham of solid appearances, we find ourselves interested and charmed.

The streets are narrow and cross one another at right angles. The houses are of one and two stories, flush with the sidewalks, and in the business sections, cage-like balconies hang out from the second stories, so that you are shielded from the sun as you pass along the streets. Spanish style of architecture prevails, and in the inner courts of many of the residences one catches glimpses of beautiful flowers in great profusion.

In the centre of Lima, as in all Spanish-American towns, is a plaza, or public square, with a fountain and statuary in the centre, and the President's Palace, the cathedral, the archbishop's residence, the municipal offices, and and other public institutions facing its four sides.

The cathedral here, the corner-stone of which is said to have been laid by Francisco Pizarro (the founder of Lima), in 1540, is one of the finest sights in Lima, and is of impressive and beautiful architecture, with two massive towers that can be seen for miles around. What pass for the bones of Pizarro are still preserved in this cathedral, and on the payment of a small tip the monks are always ready to exhibit them. This cathedral of Lima is looked upon as one of the most beautiful churches in South America.

The city has long been famed for its educational institutions; the national university, chartered in 1551, is the oldest university in America. The national library, founded in 1822, with some books from older libraries, was destroyed in 1880 by the Chileans. It contained then about 60,000 volumes. It now contains about 50,000 volumes. There are several other libraries in the city, also several technical schools, professional, classical, naval, military, and about 100 elementary schools.

At the time of the war between Peru and Chile, the city capitulated without any resistance, and the Chileans kept possession for about two years.

In addition to her many churches, Lima can make the proud boast of being the birthplace and home of the only American saint in the calendar. This is "Santa Rosa de Lima," who was canonized in 1668.

What seems to be a national costume of the ladies of Lima is the "manta." The manta is a shawl of black China crape and the amount of silk embroidery upon it indicates the wealth of the wearer. It is square in shape and about two yards in size. It is folded so as to be triangular, and the centre of the fold is placed upon the forehead, where there is usually a bit of lace that hangs down to the eyes. One end of the manta falls down to the front of the dress as far as the knee, while the other is thrown around the shoulders and fastened at the breast with an ornamental pin. The manta is worn by every woman, regardless of her rank or wealth, whenever she appears upon the street.

Lima has considerable manufacturing industries and is developing rapidly. The population is said to be about 120,000.

There are quite a number of our countrymen in Lima, and those who were fortunate enough to be allowed ashore have nothing but praise of the way they were treated.

While at Callao, the company that controls the Oroya Railroad gave an excursion up the railroad to the officers and about ninety men of the U. S. S. Tennessee on November 11th, and as we were coaling at the time none of us were able to go, much to our regret, as this railroad is one of the greatest feats of engineering ever accomplished. This railroad, which was planned and partly executed by the American engineer, Henry Meiggs, reaches an altitude of about 16,000 feet, the highest of any railroad on earth; it affords communication with the Cerro de Pasco Mining District, where is situated one of the richest copper mines in the world, controlled almost entirely by American capital.

In places over this railroad you can see the track you have traveled over in eight different stages below. In another place along this road three tunnels, one above the other, go through the same mountain. In comparison with this, the much advertised "Horseshoe Bend," and other engineering feats in railway construction in the United States, pale into insignificance.

At about 6:00 p. m., Thursday, December 12th, we got underway for Acapulco, Mexico, and after a very smooth and pleasant trip, arrived there at 12:35 p.m., Thursday, December 19th.

On entering the harbor of Acapulco, we found the Pacific Mail Steamer "City of Para" in port, and when the Flagship saluted the port, all the passengers on board the mail steamer hurried on deck and cheered both ships.

A small liberty party left the ship about noon of the 21st, and nearly all were ready to return on board long before their shore leave was up.

Acapulco is one of the principal sea ports of Mexico, with an excellent harbor; but the town itself is very disappointing. It is small, much smaller than any of us thought after looking at the prominent place it has on our maps. The population numbers about 6,000, mostly of mixed blood, the Indian and negro races predominating. There are a few Americans and Europeans, who carry on most of the exporting and importing trade of the place.

Near the centre of the town is a small plaza. In this plaza is erected a music stand where the bands from this ship and the "Tennessee" entertained the populace with music on alternate days.

Acapulco is composed of cheap buildings, dirty and poorly kept streets, sun, pineapples, gambling, and grog shops. "Monte" is openly played on the streets, and cock-fights are held on Sundays. There is supposed to be a good market in the place, but it was impossible to obtain, at any price, even enough turkeys and chickens for the crew's Christmas dinner. Coal facilities are fairly good, however, and that is about all that can be said in favor of this hot, dirty, and uninteresting place.

We left Acapulco Sunday, December 22nd, at about 3:00 p. m., bound for Pichilinque Bay, Mexico. We kept land in sight almost the entire trip, and anchored in Pichilinque Bay, at about nine, Christmas morning.

The United States Government has established a naval coal depot in Pichilinque harbor, which, though small, is one of the best harbors on the coast, being well protected on all sides. Here we found the Collier "Caithness" waiting for us.

Christmas day was spent very pleasantly by all hands. Boat races, deck sports and boxing being in order. The next day we prepared the ship for coaling, and early on the morning of the 27th we started coaling, and finished at about 8:20 a. m., of the 28th. At 11:00 a. m., the same day we left Pichilinque for Magdalena Bay, Mexico, where we arrived at 11:45 the next morning.

(Our Cruise will be continued in next issue.)

On January 1st, in accordance with instructions from the Commander-in-Chief, United States Pacific Fleet, Rear Admiral U. Sebree, U. S. Navy, assumed command of the Second Division, First Squadron, United States Pacific Fleet, consisting of the U. S. S. Tennessee (Flagship), U. S. S. Washington, U. S. S. California, and U. S. S. South Dakota, which ship will be assigned to the Second Division later.

An Expedient in Navigation.

A sailor named Taylor was wrecked on a whaler—the sea was about to prevail,
When lucky for Taylor the foundering whaler caught up with a slumbering whale.
"In order to sail her to harbor,"said Taylor, "myself I'll avail o' this gale."
So Taylor, the sailor, the sail o' the whaler did nail o'er the tail o' the whale.—*Life*.

THE WASHINGTON MONTHLY.

Printed and Published on board
U. S. S. WASHINGTON.

Vol. 1.   February, 1908.   No. 3.

Editor:
W. Rappeport, Chief Yeoman.

Printers:
J. E. Hayes, Printer.
E. F. Doherty, Ordinary Seaman.

The Washington Monthly will be published on or about the first of each month.

Price per copy, 10 cents.

Devoted to the interests of the enlisted men of the United States Navy.

Entered at "The Scuttle-Butt" as Special First-class matter.

We have recently noticed a great deal of criticism from time to time, in certain newspapers and periodicals, concerning alleged defects in vessels of the Navy. Nearly all of this criticism appears to have been written by sensational writers whose principal qualifications for writing these articles are ignorance, exaggeration, and lack of truth.

In the war with Spain, our Navy astonished the world by victories, more overwhelming and complete than there is record of in history. How we managed to make this glorious showing, if these criticisms are correct, we are at a loss to explain. Since that time our Navy has leaped to the second Naval Power of the world, and has increased in efficiency, especially in target practice, to an extent that is little short of miraculous.

Our Navy always has done what it undertook, and it will continue to do so. When Rear Admiral Evans arrives on this coast with his magnificent fleet, on time and in good condition, and is joined by the ships already here, the United States will have assembled a fleet, that in strength can be excelled only by England, and equalled by no other Power; and in its efficiency surely not excelled by any nation on earth.

It may interest our readers to have the opinion of a foreign naval expert on our Navy. Referring to certain comparative tables, he says:

"The **extraordinary** high figures for the United States ships afford food for considerable thought, for both in ships with high-powered guns or impervious to vital injury at long range the United States fleet is superior to any other navy in the world. Even by the inclusion of 40-caliber 12-inch types, extinct so far as new ships are concerned, the United States Navy is an extremely good second, and the corresponding lead in invulnerability outside of 7,000 yards is considerably increased."

"A Sad Accident"

It is with the greatest regret that we have to announce the first death that has occurred on this ship since the starting of this paper.

At about 9:30 a. m., January 14th, while this ship was coaling from the U. S. Naval Collier "Saturn," W. H. Williams, ordinary seaman, who was engaged at the time in landing bags on the superstructure deck of this ship, was caught in the coaling gear and dragged over the side of the ship, directly over the hold of the collier. Another bag of coal coming up from the collier's hold at this time, struck Williams, causing him to fall into the hold, a distance of about thirty feet. He was picked up unconscious, and brought aboard the ship, where he died from his injuries about two hours later. He was buried the following day, with full military honors, in a quiet little cemetery at Magdalena.

Williams enlisted February 9, 1907, and joined this ship at Newport, R. I., June 12, 1907. During the time he was on board this ship his conduct has been exemplary, and since entering the naval service he has had a clear record. He had a bright, cheeerful disposition, and a splendid character. He was respected by the officers and very popular among all the crew.

The WASHINGTON MONTHLY extends to his relatives and friends the deepest sympathy of the crew, who mourn the loss of a shipmate and friend.

In a recent issue of the ARMY & NAVY REGISTER, it is stated that at the request of the Bureau of Navigation of the Navy Department, the Postmaster General will recommend to Congress the enactment of legislation which shall authorize naval paymasters to issue postal money orders to enlisted men in the same manner as is done at the various post offices all over the country. This will be of practical advantage to those who send money home and will save the cost of having government checks cashed.

"The Men Behind The Guns"

A cheer and salute for the Admiral, and here's to the Captain bold,
And never forget the Commodore's debt when the deeds of might are told!
They stand to the deck through the battle's wreck when the great shells roar and screech——
And never they fear when the foe is near to practice what they preach:
But off with your hat and three times three for Columbia's true-blue sons,
The men below who batter the foe—the men behind the guns!

Oh, light and merry of heart are they when they swing into port once more,
When, with more than enough of the "green-backed stuff," they start for their leave-o'-shore;
And you'd think, perhaps, that the blue-bloused chaps who loll along the street
Are a tender bit, with salt on it, for some fierce "mustache" to eat—
Some warrior bold, with straps of gold, who dazzles and fairly stuns
The modest worth of the sailor boys—the lads who serve the guns.

But say not a word till the shot is heard that tells the fight is on,
Till the long, deep roar grows more and more from the ships of "Yank" and "Don,"
Till over the deep the tempests sweep of fire and bursting shell,
And the very air is a mad Despair in the throes of a living hell;
Then down, deep down, in the mighty ship, unseen by the midday suns,
You'll find the chaps who are giving the raps —the men behind the guns!

Oh, well they know how the cyclones blow that they loose from their cloud of death,
And they know is heard the thunder-word their fierce ten-incher saith!
The steel decks rock with the lightning shock, and shake with the great recoil,
And the sea grows red with the blood of the dead and reaches for his spoil—
But not till the foe has gone below or turns his prow and runs,
Shall the voice of peace bring sweet release to the men behind the guns!——*Rooney.*

⚜ ⚜ ⚜

Extra Compensation For Enlisted Men of the Marine Corps.

We quote the following extract from General Order No. 58, which no doubt will be of interest to the enlisted men of the Marine Corps on board: "When enlisted men of the Marine Corps are regularly detailed as signalmen by the commanding officer of any vessel of the Navy, and serve at least one month in that capacity, they shall, during the time of said service, receive the same compensation in addition to their monthly pay as is now or may hereafter be allowed enlisted men of the Navy under like circumstances."

Our New 20,000 Ton Battleships.

A great deal has been written of our new 20,000 ton battleships, "Delaware" and "North Dakota," and the following are the general dimensions and features of these vessels as embodied in the last annual report of the Chief of Bureau of Construction and Repair:

Length on load water line,   510 feet
Breadth, extreme, at load water line,
    85 ft, 2 5-8 ins.
Displacement on trial, not more than,
    20,000 tons
Mean draft to bottom of keel at trial displacement (about) 27 ft.
Total coal-bunker capacity (about)   2,300 tons
Coal carried on trial,   1,000 tons.
Feed water carried on trial   66 tons
Speed on trial,   21 knots
ARMAMENT:
    Main battery——
        Ten 12-inch breech-loading rifles.
    Secondary battery——
        Fourteen 5-inch rapid-fire guns.
        Four 3-pounder saluting guns.
        Four 1-pounder semi-automatic guns.
        Two 3-inch field pieces.
        Two machine guns, caliber, .30
    Two submerged torpedo tubes.

The arrangement of the main battery guns is such as to permit a broadside fire 25 per cent greater than that of the broadside fire of any battleship now built, or so far as is known, under construction.

The contract for the "Delaware" was placed with the Newport News Shipbuilding Company, Newport News, Va., on August 6, 1907, at a price of $3,987,000, to be completed in thirty-six months. The contract for the "North Dakota" was placed with the Fore River Shipbuilding Company, Quincy, Mass., on the same day, at a price of $4,377,000, to have Curtis turbine engines, and to be completed within thirty-four and one-half months.

On January 12th, the U. S. S. Chicago, commanded by Commander Robert M. Doyle, arrived at Magdalena Bay, from San Diego, and the following day got underway again, bound for Hampton Roads, Va., via the Straits of Magellan.

Owing to the increase in the midshipmen, it will be necessary to have an additional vessel for the annual practice cruise, and in consequence the "Chicago" will be attached to the practice squadron at the Naval Academy next summer.

Our Preliminary Target Practice.

Shortly after our arrival at Magdalena Bay, preparations were begun for the preliminary target practice. Routine drills were suspended, sub-calibre ("Ping Pong") practice, loading and other gun drills being the order of the day.

At about 7:35 a. m., of January 7th, the "Washington" got underway for the target range, and after several trial runs over the range commenced the target practice at about 10:30 a. m.

The entire 3-pounder, 6-inch and 10-inch batteries, and the port 3-inch battery were fired during the day, on the 7th, 8th, 9th and 10th, respectively. Night practice was had with the starboard 3-inch battery, from 6:40 p.m. of the 10th, to 12:50 a. m. of the 11th. During this night practice all the searchlights were kept trained on the targets, and the ammunition used was fitted with night tracers, which enabled one to follow the shells in their flight through the air.

All the men worked well and faithfully at their various stations, and the ship's company may well be proud of the record they made. While we have not got the official reports to hand, it is believed that this ship made about 80 per cent of hits, which, taking into consideration that this is the first time this ship has fired, and also that many of our guns' crews are new to the Service, this is a most remarkable record, and as good as, if not better than, any other ship on her first preliminary practice ever made before.

"The Half=Hundred Social Club"

On January 22nd a meeeting was held in the forward torpedo room to organize a social club on board ship, not exceed fifty members, and to be known as "The Half-Hundred Social Club." The object of the club is to entertain what friends they make ashore, and to promote entertainments on board ship. Should this club prove a success, it is possible that more members may be accepted.

The following named men were elected to office: President, A. Erickson, S. C. 1c. Vice-president, C. B. Murray, Elec. 1c. Secretary, E. Hayes, Cox. Treasurer, J. P. Rafferty, Elec. 3c. Asst. Treasurer, C. W. Wright, Yeo. 3c. Master of Ceremonies, E. J. Lacey, Sea. Asst. Master of Ceremonies, J. B. Hovelman, Cox.

The people on the Pacific coast are making great preparations for celebrating the coming of the Atlantic fleet, and at Mare Island special provisions are being made in anticipation of the work which is destined to be required, to a greater or less extent, on the battleships, destroyers, and other vessels.

"Cruise of the "Big Four" to Southern California"

While our stay at Magdalena Bay has been a monotonous one, and a hard one, preparing for target practice, it is at least consoling, especially now that the end is in sight, to read of the receptions tendered the First Division at the various ports they stopped at during their cruise to Southern California.

The majority of us have been speculating for sometime past, as to what sort of a reception our ship's company will receive when we once more set foot on terra firma of good old "U. S. A." The reports from the "Big Four" are reassuring and shows us that the people on the west coast are still living up to their reputation for open-handed hospitality.

Minstrel shows and dances were given ashore at Santa Barbara and at Long Beach; and, at Redondo the people of that place and of Redondo Beach extended an invitation to the crews of the vessels of the First Division to attend a Reception and Ball, which was accepted by a great many, and a very pleasant evening was enjoyed by all.

The various Electric Railway Companies were also very generous in giving the men complimentary tickets to Los Angeles, thus giving them an opportunity to visit that beautiful city. During the cruise of the "Big Four" to Southern California, the people at the various ports visited did their utmost to make their stay as pleasant as possible, and from all reports the men have nothing but praise of the way they were treated.

THE HISTORY OF A KNOCKER

A knocker knocked through all his life; when but a child at play
He knocked the little ones who helped him while the time away.
At school he knocked the other boys, and when he older grew
He knocked the fellows whom the girls smiled at as maidens do.
He never had a pleasing word to say of anyone
Who was'nt present when he spoke, he gave good cheer to none;
He rose up from his bed to knock, he knocked through all the day;
At night he knocked and piously fell on his knees to pray.

One day he knocked upon a gate--St. Peter sat inside;
"Why come you here?" the gray saint asked The man who knocked replied:
"I never killed, I never stole, I never even swore,
I always said my prayers each day; please let me in therefore."
"You cannot come," replied the saint; "but many leagues below
You'll find another gate to which immense crowds daily go;
I care not that you never stole, nor that you prayed each day---
Down there no knocker ever knocked and then was turned away."

Third Performance of the U. S. S. Tennessee Minstrel Troupe.

On the evening of January 3rd, there was a merry gathering on board the U. S. S. Tennessee, where a large number of men from all the ships present assembled to witness the third performance of the U. S. S. Tennessee Minstrel Troupe. F. T. Walling acted as interlocutor, and the end men were H. R. Renner, S. Weinstein F. B. Wigart and E. M. Mounts. Six songs were introduced in the first part, and they were all well rendered.

The second part opened up with a Hebrew monologue by L. C. Simmel. A. H. Pettibone and J. Thomas were very clever in a cross-fire conversation act, and they were followed by J. J. Egan and J. V. Madison in "Widow O' Tool's Courtship." Madison made a very creditable showing as the "Widow," and Egan as the Irish beau, simply acted natural. A. A. Achauer and B. E. Wirth as the "Jew and Ham-O-Let," were very good, and T. J. Ward, A. H. Pettibone, and H. R. Renner in "Here, There, and Everywhere," took the boys by storm with their witty stories and parodies. The show ended with a one-act farce entitled "Dutch Justice." The performance as a whole was exceptionally good. Music was furnished by the ship's orchestra, under the leadership of F. A. Varalla.

"Good Times In Store"

As it is expected that this ship will go to Puget Sound Navy Yard in the near future, for repairs, and in all probability remain there most of the coming summer it will be of interest to know how one may spend his liberty on shore to the best advantage.

First of all the Navy Yard is situated inland on the Sound, about 140 miles from the Pacific, and occupies one of the many beautiful spots of the surrounding country.

The town of Bremerton is situated at the East entrance of the Yard, and has a population of about 6,000. The town of Charleston at the West entrance, or about 1-½ miles from Bremerton, has a population of about 2,000, while Sidney, formerly known as Port Orchard, is situated just across the bay, and has a population of about 4,000.

The city of Seattle, the largest city in the State of Washington, is connected with the Navy Yard and surrounding towns by a line of steamers which operate a two hour service and make the trip (16 miles) in forty-five minutes.

The city of Tacoma, which is 30 miles further up the Sound, may be reached by street car or steamer from Seattle. Other numerous parks and suburbs of Seattle are within an hours ride from the centre of the city.

Hunting, fishing, and camping parties has in the past been the most popular sport of the officers and men who have been at the Yard during the summer months. Such parties may be gotten together for a two or three day, or even a week's outing, at a very small expense and very little exertion, as one is only required to go three or four miles up the Sound, or inland, to find almost total wilderness, and be in the midst of the towering fir forests. There is any amount of good fishing and hunting to be had, even at this close range; but if large game is expected, such as bear or deer, it will require a day's tramp into the heart of the woods to find it.

Those socially inclined will always find ample amusement, as men in uniform are always welcome to the weekly or monthly club dances or socials once they make themselves acquainted.

Seattle affords the usual run of amusements that is to be found in any of the Eastern cities, such as theatres (five in number), roller skating, beaches, parks, etc.

In concluding, it may be well to suggest for the benefit of those who smoke cigarettes, to lay in your supply before reaching the State of Washington, as the Anti-Cigarette Law is in force there. There is no restriction to smoking cigarettes, but they cannot be bought in the State.

Our Vaudeville Troupe is practicing steadily, and the next performance will in all probability be given at the Bremerton Navy Yard, upon our arrival there. From all reports they are getting into excellent shape, and a good show is promised.

We have been favored with the January issue of "THE DITTY BOX," published on board the U. S. S. West Virginia, and "THE GRAND CANON," published on board the U. S. S. Colorado. Both are neat, entertaining, creditable ship's papers, and have been running successfully for sometime past. THE WASHINGTON MONTHLY extends to them the best wishes for a continued success.

On the evening of January 28th, our Executive Officer, Lieutenant Commander James G. Doyle, having arrived to the rank of Commander, was given a dinner by the Wardroom Officers of this ship, to which the Division Commander, Captains of the "Tennessee" and "Washington," and the Executive Officer of the "Tennessee" were invited.

There is no florist in this vicinity, and the shores are apparently devoid of all vegetation; but with the aid of cactus and a few such greens as could be obtained from shore, the decoration of the table was both novel and attractive.

On January 19th, the "Washington" baseball team met defeat at the hands of the U. S. S. Tennessee, by the score of 8 to 2. This score does not by any means show that it was a one-sided game, for indeed it was not. The score stood 2 to 2, until the seventh inning, when a few safe hits, combined with a little hard luck on the "Washington's" side, gave the game to the "Tennessee."

Since then the editor has heard a few remarks regarding dissatisfaction among some of the team, which we must say is the wrong spirit to show. Do not feel discouraged over defeat, for defeat sometimes is better than victory, as it shows the weak places. It is hoped that you will all do your best to make the team a success which can be done if all pull together.

It has been learned that the Pacific coast cities are full of good amateur baseball teams who are always anxious to play the Navy.

SPECIAL BY LEASED WIRE--??

Rio de Janeiro, Jan. 12th: "Fighting Bob Evans to-day led his magnificent fleet of sixteen battleships into the harbor of Rio, and the beautiful sheet of blue water is dotted with the pride of the United States Navy. Never have the natives of the city witnessed such a magnificent array of fighting ships, myriads of flags and emblems. The entire city is crazy with delight. Fully 100,000 persons jammed every available nook and cranny near the waterfront to see the Yankee ships steam into port. From the thousands of Brazilian throats came the shouts of frenzied welcome, and back from the long line of white ships came the resounding cheers from the American sailors."

Ratings, Transfers, etc., since January First.

RATINGS:—J. Shottroff, Boatswain's Mate 2nd class, to Boatswain's Mate 1st class. J. J. Gray, Gunner's Mate 1st class, to Turret Captain 1st class. M. E. Thibodaux and A. H. Shaub, Quartermasters 3rd class, to Quartermasters 2nd class. H. Natalo, Fireman 2nd class, to Ship's Fitter 2nd class. F. Stevenson, J. G. Harner, and F. Martin, Seamen, to Coxswains. H. Smith, Seaman, to Yeoman 3rd class. W. Allen, R. L. Brooks and A. P. Hill, Mess Attendants 3rd class, to Mess Attendants 2nd class.

TRANSFERS:— Jan. 3rd, S. L. G. Pletcher, Ordinary Seaman, to Mare Island Hospital, via the "California." Jan. 13th, S. J. Peters, Hospital Steward, to the U. S. S. Chicago. Jan. 17th, F. F. Hill, Ordinary Seaman, to Mare Island Hospital, via the "Saturn."

RECEIVED:— Jan. 13th, W. T. Gildberg, Hospital Steward, from the U. S. S. Chicago.

DISCHARGED:— Jan. 13th, H. Smith, Yeoman 3rd class. Jan. 17th, F. Martin, Seaman. (Both of these men re-enlisted the day following their discharge).

DIED:—Jan. 14th, W. H. Williams, Ordinary Seaman.

SHORT ARM JOLTS.

We understand that "Bush," who recently received a bag of mail, has broken all records in the mail line. Correspondence School students and mining investment artists will have to hustle to beat his record.

Good for you "Reggie," you did your best; but the gun was not made to fire two shells.

We hear that the race boat coxswain has smelled a "rat."

The members of No. 71 mess wish to congratulate one of its members as being the only man in that mess who keeps them informed of the doings of their shipmates.

Overheard on the superstructure deck:— "No, steam beer in 'Frisco is as cold, if not colder than, the beer in New York."

"Tim" and "Gene" went fishing one bright sunny day,
And took off their shoes for comfort they say;
The sun chuckled and grinned as it shone on their feet
So dainty and small, so white and so neat.
The next morning the ship was thrilled by the news,
That these petty officers could'nt wear their shoes;
Then over their feet these two men did toil
With water, vaseline, cold cream and oil;
They grinned at each other and yelled out in pain,
"Go fishing in bare feet?—No; never again" !!!

Our painter says the best way to remove paint is to "buck" up against it before it is dry.

Mystery! Who stole the can of limburger cheese? The detective employed says he is "strong on the scent."

"Windy" Mc F's batting average is pretty high, but W. E. G. is not very far behind. We are informed that "Willie Westinghouse" is working out a scheme that will settle all doubt as to who is the champion in the Marine Compartment.

The patent for the "sky-hook" has been received on board.

"Echoes from the Tennessee"

Snodgrass, "the wise man from the west," is still handing out the "con."

If three certain men were put on diminished rations for a few days, the other members of mess forty-four would be able to get something to eat.

Volz, of the electrical department, is still looking for the "boomerang" on the mainmast.

The race boat keeper is still fooling them with "his last dime"—and he dearly loves fruit.

Intercepted wireless telegram, from Point Loma, Cal., Feb. 2nd:--"Harry K. Thaw acquitted by the jury of the murder of Stanford White, on the ground of insanity. King Carlos of Portugal, and the Crown Prince, were assassinated by anarchists."

Book Three

Vol. 1   **THE VOLUNTEER**   No. 1

February, 1908

MOTTO:
"Caelum, non animum
mutant qui trans mare
currunt"

 **Published Monthly on Board the U. S. S. Tennessee**

GREETING
To Our Readers

IN publishing **The Volunteer** to represent our ship,
We are urged on by the feeling keen to each
That nearly every man-of-war that fights for Uncle Sam
And almost every hamlet on the beach,
Has a little news sheet of some kind to represent its fame—
So why should we be quite behind the times.
We feel it but our duty now to get into the game,
Thus we've made a bold attempt to fall in line.

It is the truth—we're amateurs, but friends do not be rude
And criticise too harshly to begin.
As we age we'll try improvements that our readers may suggest,
And hope, by that, their confidence to win.
We ask you just to lend a hand and give us your support
Buy **The Volunteer** wherever you may be,
And we'll TRY to give the Tennessee the best newspaper out—
Or at least the best one published on the sea.

The VOLUNTEER

Vol. 1. Magdalena Bay, Mexico, February, 1908. No. 1.

Our Admiral

REAR ADMIRAL URIEL SEBREE, U. S. Navy, was born at Fayette, Missouri, Feb. 20, 1848. Entered the Naval Academy, July, 1863. Graduated June, 1867. Commissioned Ensign, March, 1869; Master, 1870; Lieutenant, 1871; Lieutenant-Commander, 1889; Commander, 1897; Captain, 1901, and Rear Admiral, July, 1907.

Served on board the "Canandaigua," European Station, 1867 to February, 1869; on sailing sloop "Cyane" and steamer "Saranac," Pacific Station, from July, 1869, to December, 1872; steamer "Tigress," Polaris Arctic Relief Expedition, the summer of 1873; monitor "Dictator," January to April, 1874; U. S. Flagship "Franklin," European Station, April, 1874, until January, 1877; Torpedo Station, summer of 1877; in Coast Survey on steamer "Bache," and in command of schooner "Silliman" and steamer "Gedney" from April, 1878, until July, 1881; U. S. S. "Brooklyn" (old Brooklyn), South Atlantic Station, about October, 1881, until September, 1882; Naval Academy, December, 1882, to June, 1883; command of steamer "Pinta," July, 1883, to October, 1883; steamer "Powhattan," December, 1883, to April, 1884; U. S. S. "Thetis," on Greely Relief Expedition, April, 1884, to September, 1884; Naval Academy, October, 1884, to September, 1885; Light House Inspector, Portland, Oregon, September, 1885, to September, 1889; Executive Officer, U. S. S. Baltimore, in Europe and coast of Chili, January, 1890, to March, 1892; Assistant Light House Inspector, New York, September, 1892, to July, 1893; Naval Academy, Head of Department of Seamanship, July, 1893, to October, 1894; in charge of ships at Naval Academy, October,

1894, to July, 1896; Command of U. S. S. Thetis, surveying coast of Lower California, July, 1896, to July, 1897; Command of gunboat Wheeling, on Pacific Station and in Alaska, August, 1897, to November, 1898; Light House Inspector, San Francisco, Cal., November, 1898, to October, 1901; Commandant, Naval Station, Tutuila, Samoa, November, 1901, to February, 1903; Command of U. S. S. Wisconsin, China Station, February, 1903, to January, 1904; Naval War College and Member of Board of Inspection and Survey, June, 1904, to November, 1904; Naval Secretary, Light House Board, November, 1904, to September 30, 1907; Command of Special Service Squadron (Tennessee and Washington), October 8, 1907, hoisting flag on Tennessee; assumed command of Second Division, United States Pacific Fleet, consisting of Tennessee, Washington, California and South Dakota (to be assigned) on January 1, 1908.

Our Captain

CAPTAIN T. B. HOWARD, U. S. Navy, was born August 10, 1854, at Galena, Illinois. Appointed Midshipman at Naval Academy by General U. S. Grant, June, 1869; graduated Naval Academy, May, 1873; Ensign, July, 1874; Master, January, 1879; Lieutenant, Junior Grade, 1883; Lieutenant, 1885; Lieutenant-Commander, 1889; Commander, June, 1902; Captain, February, 1907. Served on board Alaska, Wabash and Franklin (European Station) and at Key West (Virginius trouble), 1873-1875; Constellation, 1877; Plymouth, 1878-79; Kearsarge, 1879-81; Dale, 1881; Saratoga, 1884-87; Bennington, 1891-93; Commanded Caravel Pinta from Barcelona to Havana, September, 1892, to March, 1893; served on board Miantonomoh, 1893-94; Monongahela, summer, 1895; Concord, 1897-98; Charleston, 1899; Monadnock, February and March, 1900; served on board Scindia, April to August, 1900; Head of Department Ordnance and Gunnery, Naval Academy, 1901-02; Command of Puritan at Inauguration, 1901; Chesepeake, summer 1901; Nevada, 1903-05; Head of Ordnance and Gunnery, Naval Academy, 1905-07; Commanded Olympia and Naval Academy Practice Squadron, summer 1907; ordered to Command Tennessee, October 7, 1907, and assumed command on that day.

At Manila Bay, May 1, 1898, August 13, 1898, February 4-5, 1899; Subig, July 7, 1898; assisted Army at Cebu in Charleston, July, 1899, and in Monadnock, September, 1899.

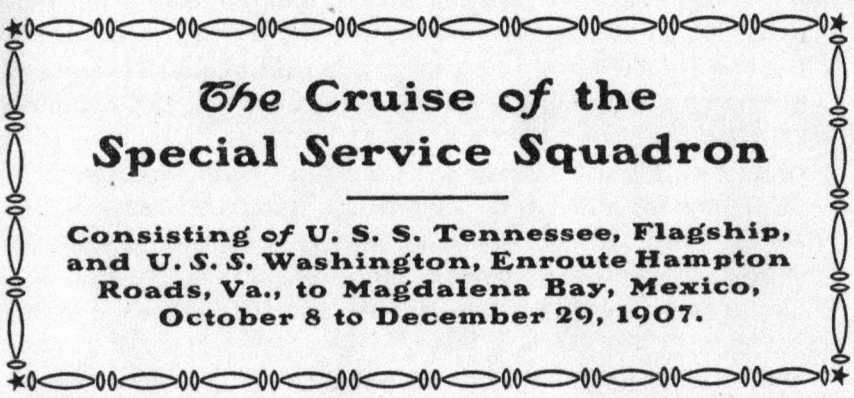

The Cruise of the Special Service Squadron

Consisting of U. S. S. Tennessee, Flagship, and U. S. S. Washington, Enroute Hampton Roads, Va., to Magdalena Bay, Mexico, October 8 to December 29, 1907.

"Full speed ahead," the Admiral said; "get everything ship-shape"
'Tis for the Barbary Coast we're bound, via Magellan's Straits.
So from that dear old Hampton Roads we headed out to sea,
A little chesty, naturally—most any one would be,
For 14,000 miles of fun in Uncle Sam's good ships
Is certainly a luxury the best of folks might wish.
Land lubbers say it's not all joy, but they don't know I swear,
For sitting by the kitchen hearth ne'er gets them any where.
We headed for the sunny South, leaving our cherished homes;
"Shift into white," the order came, as we battled with the foam.
Three charming days we pushed ahead, an uneventful trip,
Till the look-out bellowed "Land, Oh!"—still it looked more like a ship.
Who could blame that blooming sea-dog with his corvette long ago
As heaving to to blaze away, he made a holy show.
For instead of being a treasure ship, as the crazy Frenchman thought
It was but that weather-beaten spot known world wide as Sail Rock.
Ah! grand St. Thomas' soon abeam, and Culebra, too, Oh! my—
Rather than spend a season there, I think I'd sooner die.
Four winters past old Target Bay, and THAT Great Harbor, too,
Had been the only pesky things our fleet had had to view.
Culebra one fond farewell, of you we've seen enough.
A land too mean to own a town—I tell you, boys, it's tough.
Monotony is all it breeds. Who wouldn't kind of boast,
In the Special Service Squadron bound for the Pacific Coast.

Soon in that far famed Carribean with its handsome string of Isles,
We ploughed along at a 10 knot clip. It almost made me smile
Just to think of Cook's famed tourists, digging down for hundreds, right
While the Special Service Squadron gets paid to see the sight.
Lubbers say 'tis through a port-hole that we get these famous views—
We admit it, but we're better off, for we can "hold our stew;"
We enjoy the thing and draw our "dough," as we can stand the seas
While the tourist in his state-room courtesies on bended knees
And asks the hand that guides us all to take him safely home;
Then he makes a solemn heart felt vow, "On no more seas to roam."
"Good-bye, old boy." What! did not answer?" Well, he's too sick to move.
Forget him as he fades away. St. Pierre comes into view—
Simultaneously a feeling sad creeps through each fellow's mind
As we see where once a city stood, but now there's left behind
Some rubbish here, a bare place there, that a few short years before
Was as fair a little city as slept on any shore.
As we bowl along, on our port side we view the handsome coast;
Drink in the pretty scenery to regret when it is lost.
"What's that ahead?" "Why Trinidad," that blooming English Isle;
"We'll stop there sure," the Bosun said; the second section smiled.
It was their liberty day you know, and they could go ashore
In old King Ned's possession where they'd never been before.
Sure enough, the signal came: "500 hits the beach,"
To mingle with the Britishers—it blamed near made me screech.
"They handed me a lemon," I heard that some where before
But hardly realized the truth until I struck that shore.
'Twas Port of Spain they told me that this "lemon" town was named
The only thing that I could see for which the place was famed
Was a 50 per cent advance in price, which caught us fellows right
And it lasted till the Squadron went steaming out of sight.
"We're three days out," the Bosun said, "two more'n we'll cross the line,
Now boys, when Neptune boards us you'll have to come to time."
And then a fourth division boy, to show that he was bright,
Said he hoped we'd cross in daylight, as the line's not up at night.

"Go on you rook," the Bosun said; "An extra shave for that!"
You bet your boots he got it too, mixed with his royal bath.
Sure enough, just two days hence, 'bout 7 bells at night
Excitement on the forecastle gave us all a burning fright.
Long whiskered monarch of the deep and a blooming train of seven,
Came close hauled o'er the forecastle; we thought we were in heaven.
"Now, land lubbers and polly wogs, I came not here to fool,
But to-morrow morning at 8 bells, as is my Golden Rule,
I shall be back on this good ship, and with you to be frank,
I swear that I shall shave you all and duck you in the tank.
We hit our dreaming sacks that night, all strangely white from fright,
I never thought old Neptune lived until that gosh darned night.
Now by my life next morn at 8 my spine grew hot and cold,
For old Nep and his party on the forecastle stood bold.
"Where come you from and what's your game," the blooming King inquired;
"From the U. S. with 1,000 souls" the Admiral replied.
"Well by my holy polly wogs," old Nep near went insane,
"These are the biggest bally-hos to enter my domain.
That U. S. is progressing fast and soon will rule the seas,
I wot not by my dolphin's fin they'll try to capture me.
Certificates my sailor men who have crossed this line must show
For I have your name recorded in my great book down below.
By my horn spoon! Admiral Sebree! Well did I know 'twas you
For I ducked you on the "Brooklyn" in 1882.
And Hans Anderson, the Bosun's Mate, some stranger Hans, step forth,
For having ducked thee long ago, thou canst help us with the sport.
There's Manning too, master-at-arms, I have my doubts 'bout him,
But 'pears to me the safest way is let him have a swim."
So on the bridge Nep took his stand, his party strung along,
The bulls and bears began to work and gather in the throng.
The tent and tank were then put up and trouble sure did brew
As Walling tumbled down the chutes, helped out by Neptune's shoe.
"Ho! Who comes here," the judge inquired; "'Tis Fighting Doc," they said;
They rushed him up the ladder, then old Neptune lost his head.

"What fighting, screeching youth is this that dares my realm defy,
White lead for him, with sand mixed in, then plaster up his eye.
Give him green pills, my very worst, and throw him in the swim;
After a thorough ducking then throw him in again."
Poor bleeding, defiant, helpless youth—"What's left was heard to say:
"If I'd only known they wanted me, you bet I'd got away."
"Ach! Louie next," old Nep yelled out; "Sick list, sir"—Nep was wroth.
"Perhaps the sluggard's faking, and if so, bring him forth."
Then to the sick-bay rushed the bulls, some blood was to be shed,
But Louie heard them coming and covered up his head.
"Thou falsifying sluggard come forth for thy degree."
Not a leg was under Louie for some days before at sea.
While dreaming sweet beneath his bunk the ship rolled like an egg
The bunk cut loose and landed on the calf of Louie's leg.
Some boy's were quite unkind enough to yell out: "It's a fake."
But Louie swears when he gets well he'll "make dem back it take."
Then Nep leaned over to his Sec., his face seemed out of cue,
"There is some lubber on this ship, who feeds the crew on stew."
The bulls struck out and back they came—the Commissary, too
Dressed neatly from his stockings up, a polish on his shoes.
He stood bravely on the bridge, like Jackson at Bull Run,
And vainly plead with Langfield—we thought we'd lost our fun—
"You crossed the line all well enough," Langfield was heard to say
"But when father Nep sent after you, you hid yourself away."
"Ah, Ha!" the judge loudly exclaimed, "now by my holy rood,
Who passed us once in secrecy must surely get it good."
"Oh! wait, please wait!" poor Wolf yelled out; "my watch is to me tied."
"That makes no difference," said the Judge; "we'll give you both a ride."
Then down he went, and fought and kicked, and then he tried to swim,
But the bears seemed to be everywhere to keep poor Wolfie in.
After some time they pulled him out, wet, ragged and chagrined,
Then dropped him in the laundry, where they ironed him out again.
Next! Equipment Yeoman Miley appeared upon the scene
Urged to take his medicine by Quartermaster Green.

The Bosun said: "By my horn spoon, 'tis wrong to duck him so;"
The Bosun's Mate thought different though for he had been below
To bum a piece of rope yarn, a little soap or lye,
But always heard with deep chagrin the ever prompt reply:
"An order, friend, an order, and correctly signed you know."
The Judge said, "I will order now, so down the chute you go."
Into that blooming rookie's tank they dumped him legs and all
And when the bears were finished he was fished out feeling small.
So they kept up initiation till the bulls looked pretty thin,
Then the fourth division shouted throw the Neptune party in.
So down the chute old Neptune went, Judge, Sec. and all the rest;
When father Nep rose from the tank he said beneath his breath
"Now by my top de gallant sail I've boarded everything
That ever crossed this line of mine, and you mutts threw me in,
Well Davey Jones will have your bones for this fine game, now mind!"
Then shooting o'er the forecastle he left our ship behind.
'Twas rude for us to duck old Nep, but progress is the thing
While the Special Service Squadron ploughs bravely through the swim.
We shot the sun each morn and noon, we guessed at it each night,
We shot that sun so dog-gone much, it hid clean out of sight,
We did not need it anyway, we shot it just for sport.
Somebody shouted Rio and next day we were in port.
Ah! What a handsome place is this, as Sugar Loaf we pass
And resting on that world-famed Bay, the town looms up at last.
What—Liberty! and for all hands? You bet we took it in,
And everything went lovely, but our purse got mighty thin.
We rode in mule cars, electric cars, went up the mountain, too;
We visited the gardens and took in all the views.
The Avenida Central seems the finest sight that's there
But compared with our dear Broadway, why, it isn't any where.
Another fourth division boy evidently seeking fame
Says, "This town's just like old New York"—from Schenectady he came;
Another said, "Beats Rabbit Hash," that famed Kentucky town,
But Kinnicknick, Ohio, had it trimmed up all around.
A signal boy said, "I'm from Zipp;" they laughed at that kid, too
But never mind, the old U. S. will do for me or you.
We won a home in Rio and were getting quite content

(Continued on Page Nine)

We bucked it boys, and bucked it hard but what's the use to boast
Magellan bucked it long ago when he made for the coast.
We struck his Straits and 'twas no fun, that gol-derned mess of sea,
You can bet your life the waves run there 'bout high enough for me
The "Shell Backs" said, "Why that's no sea. Go on, rook, that's not high,
Why in the old Galena"—then they'd wink the other eye.
But if I listened to them "Shell Backs" they would soon make me believe
That the old time Bon Home Richard could whip our Tennessee.
Among the snow-capped mountains in that blooming pesky Strait
We dropped our hook at Sandy Point, the city built too late.
They said, " 'Twas early summer," and I hope it was by gosh,
For if summer's very much like that, it is a blooming horse.
What made me laugh till I blamed near cried, the Bandmaster at Mess
Had declared to us poor rookies, that he in white undress
Came through these same derned blooming Straits, in the good Chicago, too.
But now he quickly changed his mind and said he guessed 'twas blues.
We skipped old "Bandy" on the line, we thought he'd made the trip,
But if he went through them Straits in white 'twas in a flying ship.
The Squadron coaled in some jig time, 'twas good to get to work
For the temperature at Sandy Point would tolerate no shirk.
We hit the beach, some few of us, to verify Ballou
Who in "Equatorial America" gives such a pesky view
Of cannibals, of crooks and such, and says the town is wild;
But upon my blooming salty soul I nearly cracked a smile—
The natives there, my dear friend, upon my soul they do,
Act very ordinary, 'bout the same as I or you.
We did the town a little bit, there wasn't much to do,
Then the Special Service Squadron dug for the ocean blue.
Say, friend, 'tis cold in old "Mag's" Straits, but by my sun-burnt hide
The scenery there was just enough to set us sailor's wild.
By gosh it was right pretty too, let lubbers talk 's they like,
For in our own dear U. S. A. 'tis many a mile of hike
To find a scene compared to these fine hills, and glaciers, too;
I hope not to exaggerate—" 'Tis a mighty handsome view."

The VOLUNTEER

Published Monthly on Board the U. S. S. Tennessee

Cash, Thomas & Erwin, Publishers

Subscription......................$1.50 a Year
Single Copies......................15 Cents

Vol. 1　　　　February, 1908　　　　No. 1

"The Volunteer."

In selecting a name for a paper to represent our good ship, the "Tennessee," we have decided on THE VOLUNTEER, and quote the following historical facts, taken from the Encyclopedia Americana in reference to the State of Tennessee:

"In 1847, the volunteers of Tennessee, in the War with Mexico, won, by their valor and endurance, imperishable honors at Vera Cruz and Chapultepec. Though the requisition on Tennessee by the War Department called for three regiments, numbering in all 2,800 men, yet 30,000 volunteers tendered their services and in doing this won for Tennessee the name of "The Volunteer State."

May the U. S. S. Tennessee be ever as ready to defend the honor of our country at sea as the sons of Tennessee have ever defended the honor and glory of the nation on land.

THE VOLUNTEER feels that it is but a humble representative of one of the finest ships in our Navy, named for one of the grandest States in our Union. It is no doubt far beyond us to do justice to either, but we will always honor and reverence both.

Enough Marines.

It appears from a statement recently given out at the U. S. Marine Corps Headquarters in Washington that it will soon be as difficult to enter the Corps as to obtain a civil service position. For the first time in many years the authorized complement of 8,700 men has been recruited and the advertising for recruits is being discontinued and the offices closed. It will be difficult to increase the standard of one of the finest military bodies in the world, but it must be gratifying to be able to pick the most desirable of desirable applicants for enlistment.

The Cruise of the Special Service Squadron

(Continued from Page Seven)

When all at once a signal came and up the anchor went.
We shot the sun a few times more, I blamed near lost my count,
For the Special Service Squadron was headed for the Mount.
We made it too, you bet we did, for all good sailors can;
We anchored off the city, there was joy in every man.
Oh! ho there—well, by jingo, whose familiar face comes forth—
Lord bless me, 'tis Bottini, the father of the port.
Come on my boys, my boat is here, don't fail to hit the shore.
We'll miss our friend Bottini when we see his face no more.
It was with joy we hailed the word, "Lay aft, put your names down,"
And ride in friend Bottini's boat, he'll take you into town.
We lost no time, you bet on that, and e're it came on night
Half the Special Service Squadron was taking in the sights.
Ah yes indeed tis well worth while, we had a jolly time,
It reminded us of Boston, so far above the line.
A bull fight, boys, so came the news; we trembled some that night,
And next day hastened out to see the bulls that wouldn't fight.
A "lemon show" we thought it was, for they didn't kill the bull,
They teased him, jabbed him, taunted him, they gave his horns a pull.
We couldn't savvy such a deal, for when we pay our "mun,"
The Special Service Squadron boys pay it to see some fun.
Some guys came in, some dressed in red, some green and some in pink,
And every gosh-derned color that a human mind could think.
The crowd went wild, threw up their hats, they thought it funny, too,
But try all I could my blamed old mind wouldn't see it in that view.
Then came the bull, a fair sized cow, some vicious I suppose
But he failed at once to show it, so they whacked him on the nose;
They whacked him twice and then some more, as for the door he run.
The audience went wild with joy—I couldn't see the fun.
Well by my soul, on the fourth try they got one bull real mad,

He actually jumped up and down, and at the fighters stared.
I trembled slightly for I thought I'd surely see some fun
But my hopes were smashed to splinters, as for the door he run.
I left that place in blamed disgust, one solemn vow I made,
I'd go kill 12 John Barley Corns, then through them bulls I'd wade.
What made me madder'n some wet hen, one dago close behind,
Accused me of "no libertad, no hot blood," of his kind.
I told him Jim, I sez, sez I, "Come with me to New York,
And I'll show you plugs a fist fight that will make you lose your block"
Straightway I vowed I'd hit the ship, was feeling gol derned sore,
When I saw our good Top Sergeant Smith a hitting up the shore.
I sat myself right down to think—strange things passed through my mind,
I thought the dago might be sore 'cause I left the fight behind,
But I soon found a sympathizer, for "Sarge" had been done too;
He hesitated telling, but between I and you
He bought a lottery ticket from a blooming bunch of clay,
Who swore 'twould draw $10,000 upon the Sabbath day.
Come to find out, the lottery had drawn the day before,
So we scrambled on Bottini's tug and beat it from the shore.
The natives surely did us for about all they could do,
And then many million locusts got underway and flew
Clean across that stretch of water and landed on our ship.
They started to dislodge us and to make their home of it;
They seemed to have their nerve with them to visit us like rain,
Still they must have been land lubbers with apparent lack of brains
For as soon as we got underway, they all turned up their kicks—
Now there's 40,000,000 locusts sailing up the river Styx.
How those brave prevaricators on the forecastle will blow
That they took a locust cargo out of Montevideo.
'Twas a pleasant place in spite of that and we had a right good time,
But the Special Service Squadron had to leave the place behind.
Just three days out and by my wheel how that darn wind did blow,
It washed us clean from stem to stern, it made a holy show;
The forecastle was so tickled at a chance to buck the swell,
That the blooming ventilators upon the deck soon fell.
The Washington had so blamed much fun and o'er our fall did gloat,
That she dove into an extra sea and smashed her gosh-derned boat.

Ballou says that they wear no clothes, the natives of this land,
By my dern heart perhaps they don't, but I can't understand;
I have it now—perhaps Ballou called early in the morn,
Or met some hard luck native who had his clothes in pawn,
For when a blooming overcoat comes handy to us men,
I think that gosh derned temperature calls for something more than skin.
The "Shell Backs" moaned to think, by gosh, that Magellan in his ship
Had taken 37 days from coast to coast to slip.
But think who old Magellan was, of whom these "Shell Backs" boast,
'Long side the Special Service Ships bound for the other coast.
Ah! Soon 'twas o'er, the hills were hid, we struck the ocean blue,
And by my gosh derned bulwarks the ocean struck us, too.
We rose clean up, then sank way down, a feeling so serene,
And on every downward motion some rook would spill his beans;
Pacifico, by my port tack, means peaceful I have heard,
Tongue-tied should old Bilboa have been for muttering such a word.
'Twas peaceful, too, the "Shell Backs" said, the Galena would make play
Of such a blamed stage storm as that—I had to turn away;
Then I cussed up old Magellan and I cussed them "Shell Backs" too,
I derned the old Galena and I cussed a streak of blue.
The Albatross enjoyed it though, this weather rough and thick,
But by my shivering timbers, I couldn't, I was sick.
Well after she had rolled and bowled and dipped her gosh derned arms,
I let up in my cussing and the sea became a calm.
Then I forgave poor old Magellan when we cleared that storm of sleet
For he who tastes the bitter can appreciate the sweet.
We straightened out on our fair course, for Callao, they said,
But by my trembling weather brace, I felt like one most dead.
Mess gear was bent—bean soup said some; the ship's cook shook his spoon;
The lubber who can't scoff that soup will eat naught else this noon.
I made a rush, gol dern my soul, six feeds I'd let slip by

THE VOLUNTEER

I made one dive for a pan of soup, and was ready then to die.
By gosh, mates, that was surely fine—it touched my tender spot,
Took me back to Indiana, and that little country cot,
How I longed to see that cottage stoop, the country grocery, too,
A shrill sound from the Bosun's pipe—my dream was o'er—
    "Turn to."
We plugged away at 13 knots, and put the miles behind,
Until one day just after mess, a rumor filled the wind;
The Admiral's Coxswain,"Spring-heel Jack," the Navigating Boy,
Came forth upon the forecastle and shouted, "Land ahoy!"
"By heck, we're lost," Springy sung out; "I know we're lost,
    said he,
"For I can tell this blooming land by tasting of the sea."
We lowered him the canvas bag, he muttered as he drank
"This temperance stuff speaks but the truth—yes, lost men, to be
    frank
Peru is sunk, now hark you men, we're on the bloody Mount."
Somebody said $5.80 and Springfield took the count.
We were'nt lost though, for that blamed noon we sighted land all
    right
And close upon our starboard hand came Callao in sight.
We hoped great things of Callao and thought that with a pull
We might get to see a bull fight where the dago fought the bull.
'Twas after lunch with weary eyes we watched that signal too,
And sure enough, our hopes were dashed, "No liberty for you."
Yellow fever epidemic to keep us from the shore
We all planned on a bang-up time—I'll bet the Admiral swore
When he d sailed this Squadron miles and miles; given liberty
    enough,
To hit this gosh derned sample town; Diseases!—gee 'twas tough.
We hung about old Callao, three long days in despair,
Till the Chaplain says, "Now boys," sez he; "you see yon
    mountains there—
Tomorrow morning at three bells we'll make a pleasure trip
Up to that very highest peak and rubber at the ship."
Next morning early on the shore, three score and ten good boys
Hooked on behind an iron horse that made all kinds of noise;
We went straight up, and up and up, I thought we'd never stop,
Till the dago on the engine yelled, "all out, this is the top."
We scrambled out to look about and sized it up, then down,
And voted it a capital trip, then settled back to town.

We reached the ship and in three days we all got underway
For Acapulco for some coal, then Pichilinque Bay;
We kicked away for two long days, our faces wreathed in smiles,
When a thought struck us of turtle soup, we headed for some isles;
Gallapagos they are called, off the Ecuadorian coast,
    They are right pretty things, I swear, but of nothing else can boast.
We passed them close on our port hand, 'bout 5 o'clock that night
I kicked the skin all off my shin, no turtles were in sight.
I was somewhat disappointed too, you can guess what 'twas about
'Cause if it hadn't been for turtles we would never have gone out.
Just wait 'till I bring back to mind some of them stories told
Upon our blooming forecastle. I feared for them boys' souls.
The Master-at-Arms, I believe it was, said twenty-seven feet
Was the biggest deep-sea turtle that he had chanced to meet;
Then that blamed Indiana kid that's always butting in,
Said he had seen mock turtles that were near as big again.
My education on these things was never very great
So I went aft to the library to see what books relate.
I grabbed the Encyclopedia, which contains things near and far,
And turned the pages rapidly till I came to T-U-R.
Four hundred to six hundred pounds! By gosh I figured then
If his length was twenty-seven feet, he must be full of wind.
Mock turtles then I hunted for, but could not seem to find;
I hastened to the forecastle, strange things were in my mind.
Then by gosh darn I fell right on, what's M-O-C-K mean,
That pesky Indiana kid best not by me be seen.
So thus we steamed for Mexico, with scarcely any breeze.
I'd read a whole derned lot in books, 'bout moon light nights at sea,
But the beauty of the Southern skies, with weather always fine
    Just puts them dern land lubber authors, forty years behind the times.
We sighted Acapulco, after a very pleasant trip,
    Steamed in and came to anchor, then "turned to" and coaled the ship.
This wasn't much, this little berg, for ships like us to hit,
But we needed some black diamonds or we'd never thought of it.
So when that blooming word was passed for special first class men
Not to exceed some 25, to put down their names again,
We were in that boat in some jig time and soon were on the beach

The gringoes saw us coming and decided that they'd teach
Us poor easy Americans all 'bout some gosh derned fun,
That started with a banjo and ended with the sun.
A rose, a tree and some derned fish were also sacheted in,
I saw three big white gaming bones, then plunged right in to win.
I knew that I was breaking rules of Posey County, too,
But Deacon Jones would have done the same, for "it's do as the Romans do."
"Hands up" 's the word; "Your money down, already boys," 'twas fun;
"Banjo, rose and a lovely fish"—by cracky I had won.
That poor lone fish to me looked good, so I piled the pesos on.
He sure brought home the bacon, too, for three times straight he won.
They handed me a small sized quart of dago dollars, too,
But I saw the Chaplain coming, so up the street I flew.
I guess it's just as well I did, for while in school quite young
I never there could learn the rule on how not to get done.
The main things that they tried to teach in my small district school
Were honor bright, turn in at night, and keep the Golden Rule.
Them New York boys, though extra bright, who say their school's no joke
Failed to see the Chaplain coming, so they ended up dead broke.
That night out on the forecastle I watched the setting sun
And smiled to think I'd been ashore and returned for once unstung.
The Special Service Squadron got underway next day
And hustled off at 13 knots for Pichilinque Bay.
We dropped anchor Christmas morning and I looked to see the town,
But twist my blamed neck as I could, the dern thing wasn't round.
I thought right sure we'd made a bust, so I called for "Spring Heel Jack;"
I knew that he could tell us if we'd fallen off the track.
Springy said he thought he knew, but didn't care to tell,
As from previous navigating he had not yet gotten well.
Well, there are worse places than Mexico, but not in U. S. A.,
So we tried to thin our noodles how to make a pleasant day.
But at 8 bells old mess gear said, come boys here is your spread
In a blooming Yuletide dinner that will stand you on your head.

We did fair justice to our meal, and two strokes of the bell
Found us up on the forecastle for the sport we love so well;
So we pulled off our boat races—they were fairly good at that,
But the thing that made me laugh till I was blinder than a bat,
Was to see them blamed coal heavers climb down into the scow,
Out oars, and then give away, just as if they did know how.
"Together boys," the Coxswain cried; they straightened on the course,
The starboard stroke made one huge splash—Say man, he was a horse—
First he'd give way, then number two, then number three and four
And soon they'd make another try, the air was full of oars.
They crabbed and sawed and missed and cussed; it was a holy fright,
But they finally pulled together, at the mess table that night.
Those Newport boys in the deck-hands' boat, some of our new Cadets,
Just pulled fine stroke and raced alone, like old Galena vets.
The "Shell Backs" mustered in a bunch must have their little say
Of course the old Galena's crew would surely walk away
From anything in commission now. What must that ship have been?
They'll not hesitate to tell you—wooden ship and iron men.
We coaled the ships, cleaned up next day, and then got underway
For a place some distance around the point, called Magdalena Bay,
It belongs to Mexico, they claim here on the Tennessee,
I'm glad it does, I'd hate like time to think it belonged to me.
We made it as we'd made them all, and when the hook went down
I strolled out on the forecastle to see the blooming town.
I'm somewhat of a rural youth, and of scenery never tire,
But when I looked for Magdalena—man, I thought there'd been a fire.
The climate's fine, the bay is large, the fishing something grand,
But Mexico can keep all this, just head us for God's land.
We found the California here, she gave us thirteen guns,
We took a rest for two short days, then things began to hum,
For Admiral Dayton's mighty "Four" came steaming in from sea,
And the Special Service Squadron next day had ceased to be.
We'll always have a soft place, boys, for our old Squadron, too,
And when we anchor in our homes, our Navy life all through,
How we'll dance those youngsters on our knees and to them then relate
The Special Service Squadron voyage made through Magellan's Straits.

Our Minstrel Troupe

The following program was rendered by the Minstrel Troupe of the Tennessee to the officers and fifty men from each of the ships of the fleet present, on Friday evening, January 3, 1908. The program was very prettily put on and we extend hearty congratulations to our very able performers. We trust to hear from them again soon. The program follows:

PART 1

Opening Chorus—"Picture To-Night" .... Entire Company
"Here Come Our End Men" .... Entire Company
End Song—"Moses Andrew Jackson" .... H. R. Renner
Solo—"Beautiful Story" .... T. F. Calhoun
End Song—"Mormon Coon" .... E. M. Mounts
Solo—"Somewhere" .... W. Elliot
End Song—"Lindy Lou" .... F. B. Wigart
Solo—"Honey Boy" .... F. T. Walling
Grand Finale—"Honey Boys" .... Entire Company

Interlocuter, F. T. Walling; Tambos, H. R. Renner, S. Weinstein; Bones, F. B. Wigart, E. M. Mounts; Circle, Wrightson, Achauer, Ward, Elliot, Wolfartz, Quattle, Egan, Pritchard, Allen, Thomas, Johnson, Persing, Kelley, Calhoun, Pettibone, Cohen.

PART 2

"Goldstein's Troubles" .... L. C. Simmel
"A Little Bit of Nonsense" .... A. H. Pettibone and J. Thomas
"Widow O'Toole's Courtship" .... J. J. Egan and J. V. Madison
"The Jew and Ham-o-let" .... A. A. Achauer and B. E. Wirth
"Here, There, and Everywhere" ....
 .... T. J. Ward, A. H. Pettibone and H. R. Renner
The Tennessee Quartette, W. Elliot, F. T. Walling, H. R. Renner and J. O. Johnson

A one-act farce, entitled "Dutch Justice," was then presented, with the following cast of characters:

Judge Schnitzenberger .... A. H. Pettibone
District Attorney Soak-um .... A. Quattle
Lawyer U. B. Damn .... B. E. Wirth
Court Clerk .... J. O. Johnson
Court Officer Dooley .... J. J. Egan
A. Damn Swindler .... J. Thomas
Johnnie Gluefinger .... A. Wrightson
Lizzie Ketchum .... J. V. Madison
Terry McSwat .... J. E. Persing

Time—Present.   Place—Magdalena Bay.

Music was furnished by the U. S. S. Tennessee Orchestra.

The following staff performed their duties in a very able manner: General manager, C. H. Dickens, Chaplain, U. S. N.;

treasurer, Geo. R. Venable, Paymaster, U. S. N.; stage manager, J. F. McCarthy, Gunner, U. S. N.; secretary, B. E. Wirth; stage director, F. T. Walling; musical director, F. A. Varalla; stage carpenter, Chas. Coleman; stage electrician, John Nordmark; property man, R. J. Austin.

"In the Swim"

A recent editorial in the "Sladesville Democrat," which it is feared will have a disastrous effect on the minds of the young men from that section of the country who contemplate entering the Navy, locates Cyrus Kimbrough in the nigh official capacity of painter on the U. S. S. Tennessee, which the "Democrat" understands to be a dangerous job, as a letter recently received from "Cy" states that while engaged in duty on the target raft the boat officer of a departing cutter ordered some of the men to "throw the painter off."

Gentleman soliciting funds in the cause of temperance—"Please give something to help down drink?"

Ship's Cook—"Certainly; take several of Sunday's base-ball party.

A maid who lived in Phillie came to see the Tennessee,
She was dead in love with Meyer, or at least she seemed to be;
Bob also thought quite well of her and just to be a sport
Mailed heaps of picture post cards from almost every port.
In a recent mail a letter came, Bob grabbed it and he read
"You may keep on sending postals, but do not write—"I'm wed."

P. Flynn, our genial boatswain's mate, in discussing naval tactics, states that when the anchor is weighed for San Francisco he is of the opinion that it will not weigh the same as when that operation was performed at Pichilinque Bay.

Conumdrum: Why is Campbell, the plumber, not like an umbrella?

Answer: An umbrella will shut up.

> The last issue of the "Washington Monthly"
> Had a blot on its pages so white,
> Yet the rythm was plainly deciphered
> By holding it up to the light.
> The verse was apparently cancelled
> Because it contained something warm,
> But the blot did not "Count" as the issue sold out,
> And the "Monthly" still seems to "Lib on."

The butcher has broken out a new apron on the strength of the rumor that the 40 per cent. increase has gone through.

This is leap year, but all bachelors need not be alarmed. One apparently sure thing is that the majority of the members of the Carpenter's gang will not receive even an old maid's proposal.

Baseball

As was anticipated by previous good playing while on the Atlantic coast, our baseball team has been doing excellent work since the arrival of the Tennessee at Magdalena Bay. The following is a summary of games played during January:

```
January 2                              R  H  E
Tennessee ....................0 1 1 1 0 0— 3  5  3
California ...................0 2 2 5 1 x—10 10  3
```
Batteries—Teubert, Blahos and Gorsuch; Throwson and Higgins.
```
January 4                              R  H  E
Tennessee ....................4 2 0 2 0 1 0—9  9  3
Washington ...................0 0 0 0 0 2 2—4  3  4
```
Batteries—Blahos and Gorsuch; Maves and English.
```
January 19                             R  H  E
Tennessee ....................0 2 0 0 3 1 0 0 0—6 11  5
Washington ...................2 0 0 0 0 0 0 0 0—2  6  4
```
Batteries—Blahos and Gorsuch; Maves and English.
```
January 25                             R  H  E
Tennessee ....................3 0 3 0 0 0 0 4 x—10 16  4
Preble .......................0 0 0 1 0 2 0 1 0— 4  8  6
```
Batteries—Blahos and Gorsuch; Borgwardt and Kooneman.
```
January 28                             R  H  E
Tennessee ....................0 6 0 1 1 0 0 0 x—8 12  2
West Virginia ................0 2 0 0 0 0 0 0 2—4 11  5
```
Batteries—Blahos and Gorsuch; Schaffer, Snyder and Stanard.

The following is the line-up of the Tennessee's team: Gorsuch, c; Blahos, Rice and Teubert, p; Bush, 1b; Kelly, 2b; Riesey, 3b; Hanus, ss; Green, lf; McCafferty, cf; Zehner, rf; substitutes: Moffitt and Helreigel. In charge of team, Asst. Surgeon J. B. Kaufman; manager, R. A. Young; captain, P. H. Kelly; score-keeper, J. G. Ebert.

Much credit for the excellent showing made by the team is due to the efforts of Dr. Kaufman, Manager Young, and to the excellent pitching of Blahos. The team work appears to be improving and with more practice THE VOLUNTEER expects to record for the champion team of the Pacific Fleet.

The prestige of the Tennessee in baseball was again maintained on January 5th, when a team from the Ward-room crossed bats with the Ward-room officers of the West Virginia. The game was a hummer and resulted in a victory of 4 to 2 for the Tennessee, much credit being due Dr. Kaufman and Lt. Comdr. Robertson, the very able battery of our team. The line-up—Tennessee: Lt. Com. A. H. Robertson, c; Asst. Surg. J. B. Kaufman, p; Lt. M. J. McCormack, 1b; Lt. W. K. Wortman, 2b; Ens. J. D. Willson, 3b; Lt. J. P. Lannon, ss; Paym'r G. A. Venable, lf; Lt. W. W. Galbraith, cf; 1st Lt. E. B. Manwaring, rf. West Virginia: Capt. H. R. Lay, c; Ens. J. W. Wilcox, p; Lt. L. B. Porterfield, 1b; Maj. J. T. Myers, 2b; Lt. J. C. Fremont, 3b; Lt. Comdr. P. Symington, ss; Lt. W. H. Allen, lf; Ens. H. Kays, cf; Lt. T. A. Kittinger, rf.

Preliminary Target Practice 1908

On January 6th, the U. S. S. Washington, and on the 11th, the U. S. S. Tennessee, went on the target range at Magdalena Bay for the purpose of conducting preliminary target practice. The weather was ideal and considering that the guns had been fired but once before on the government acceptance trial, the result of the practice was exceedingly gratifying. The following table shows the "shots per gun per minute," the "hits per gun per minute," and the best pointer for each caliber:

U. S. S. TENNESSEE

	av.s.p.g.p.m.	av.h.p.g.p.m.
10-inch	1.10	.87
6-inch	6.79	4.88
3-inch (night)	9.58	5.84
3-pounder	15.87	6.05

BEST POINTERS

10-inch, D. Sullivan, Sea.	1.86
6-inch, F. D. Bell, O. S.; C. Quisenberry, O. S.	10.43
3-inch, G. C. House, O. S.	12.24
3-pounder, M. Malley, Prvt.	14.54

U. S. S. WASHINGTON

	av.s.p.g.p.m.	av.h.p.g.p.m.
10-inch	1.22	.86
6-inch	5.61	4.21
3-inch (night)	10.19	7.40
3-inch (day)	11.59	8.74
3-pounder	19.89	9.06

BEST POINTERS

10-inch, H. R. Bristol, Sea.	1.24
6-inch, J. B. Maze, Sea.	9.23
3-inch (day), T. E. King, O. S.	12.28
3-inch (night), B. Conrad, O. S.	12.50
3-pounder, W. Bednawski, Prvt.; J. J. Fox, Prvt.	15.65

At the time of going to press our ship is about to conduct her first record practice and our most sincere wish is that in our March number we may be able to credit a number of world's records to the U. S. S. Tennessee.

Itinerary—U. S. S. Tennessee

Port	Arrival	Departure	Miles
League Island, Pa. (com's'd)	July 17, '06	Nov. 1, '06	......
Hampton Roads, Va.	Nov. 3 "	" 8 "	233
Piney Point, Md.	" 8 "	" 8 "	98
Colon, Panama	" 14 "	" 15 "	1834
Chiriqui Lagoon.	" 16 "	" 16 "	130
Ponce, Porto Rico	" 21 "	" 22 "	1041
Hampton Roads, Va.	" 26 "	Dec. 16 "	1285
League Island, Pa.	Dec. 18 "	Apr. 12, '07	240
Hampton Roads, Va.	Apr. 13 '07	" 14 "	233
Lynn Haven Bay, Va.	" 14 "	" 16 "	15
Hampton Roads, Va.	" 16 "	May 16 "	16
Provincetown, Mass.	May 18 "	" 24 "	530
Boston, Mass.	" 25 "	June 5 "	53
Hampton Roads, Va.	June 7 "	" 11 "	555
Newport, R. I.	" 12 "	" 14 "	382
Royan, France	" 23 "	July 2 "	3112
Ile D' Aix, France	July 2 "	" 3 "	52
La Rochelle, France	" 3 "	" 11 "	10
Brest, France	" 12 "	" 25 "	235
Tompkinsville, S. I.	Aug. 6 "	Aug. 16 "	3194
Hampton Roads, Va.	" 17 "	" 17 "	270
Newport, R. I.	" 18 "	" 19 "	392
Boston, Mass.	" 20 "	Sept. 30 "	265
Newport, R. I.	Oct. 1 "	Oct. 4 "	265
Hampton Roads, Va.	" 5 "	" 12 "	392
Port of Spain, Trinidad	" 18 "	" 24 "	1904
Rio de Janeiro, Brazil	Nov. 4 "	Nov. 10 "	3300
Montevideo, Uruguay	" 13 "	" 19 "	1044
Punta Arenas, Chile	" 23 "	" 27 "	1325
Callao, Peru	Dec. 5 "	Dec. 12 "	2760
Acapulco, Mexico	" 19 "	" 22 "	2240
Pichilinque Bay, Mexico	" 25 "	" 28 "	785
Magdalena Bay, Mexico	" 29 "	....	315
			28,505

Have you seen this week's issue of

The Saturday Evening Post

It's Simply Great

Also, Pearson's
Munsey's
Railroad Man's
Short-Story
Motor
Cosmopolitan
Argosy
Popular
Metropolitan
The Ocean

Call and see
CLOWRY,
Quartermaster

(Look for more next month)

No. 6 Chart House Lane, Forward Bridge

The Volunteer

It is intended to publish a series of half-tones of the Tennessee, members of the crew, and interesting views which can be obtained from time to time. Owing to our inability to intelligently communicate with a base of supplies, no half-tones appear in this issue. Information concerning our ship is therefore omitted from the first issue of THE VOLUNTEER and will appear in the March number in connection with some of the half-tones referred to above.

THE EDITORS.

Dinner
U. S. S. Tennessee

San Francisco, Cal.
February 22, 1908

MENU

Clam Chowder   Crackers

Celery   Pickles

Roast Turkey with Dressing

Cranberry Sauce

Peas   Mashed Potatoes

Egg Salad

Pumpkin Pie   Mince Pie

Mixed Nuts   Oranges   Apples

American Cheese   Coffee

Cigars

BOOK FOUR

THE VOLUNTEER

Easter Number
April, 1908

San Francisco
California

Published Monthly
on Board the
U. S. S. Tennessee

To Ship and State

In our April number thee we greet
Fair land of Tennessee,
Of a name so grand few other states can boast,
No matter where our ship doth go
We hear great talk of thee—
Thy scenic beauty famed from coast to coast;
Thy mountains and thy great divides,
Fair verdue, ever green,
Thy glorious rivers noted far and wide,
Assist to give our nation
Its ever pleasing scenes.
Thy sons in history, too, live true and tried.
In honor of thy glorious deeds
Our U. S. government
Decided that thy name should once again
Be inscribed upon a cruiser
Of the best and swiftest type—
So upon our good ship now thine honored name
Appears, placed there by thine own hand
But four short years ago;
For was it not thy daughter brave and true
That christened her the Tennessee
With gold encased champagne
As the good ship plunged into the ocean blue.
We trust that both in years to come
Prosperity may share,
May the history of each eternally be
A credit to the nation
In ship as well as state,
May God always bless and keep the Tennessees.

MISS KEITH FRAZIER
Sponsor U. S. S. Tennessee

Photo by Harris & Ewing

VOL. 1   APRIL, 1908.   No. 3

CRUISING AROUND SOUTHERN CALIFORNIA

ON March 1st the Tennessee dropped anchor in the harbor of Santa Barbara, California, having left San Francisco on the 29th of February.

Santa Barbara is a city of about 8,000 population, very prettily situated on a beautiful harbor at the foot of a large group of hills, and one of the most delightful of the large number of winter resorts located in Southern California. The climate is salubrious and is strongly indicated by the large number of tourists and pleasure seekers from nearly all parts of the United States. The Potter Hotel, located near the water's edge, is a large, excellently fitted and popular hostelry. Back of the hotel is located a field of beautiful white lilies which, when in bloom, present a beautiful appearance and fill the surrounding air with a delightful odor.

Another point of interest is the Santa Barbara Mission, established in 1787, and one of the largest and oldest missions in the United States.

There is a very pretty plaza and boulevard skirting the harbor, which seems to be very popular as a driveway and walk for the citizens of the city. The moonlight nights are delightful in this locality and the sunsets are those of the glorious west.

Just outside of Santa Barbara is the measured mile standardization course laid out by direction of the Navy Department for the standardization of the propellors of naval vessels. After obtaining tactical data on the 2nd and 3rd of March, a few trial runs at 16, 18 and 20 knots speed were made on the 4th. It must indeed have been a beautiful sight presented by the Tennessee while tearing through the water at 20 knots, smoke rolling in clouds from the huge stacks. Can it be that the few who so fondly criticise ship construction realize what it means to see a ship of the Tennessee's tonnage, ploughing through the water with the speed of a race horse, machinery working splendidly, and ready for almost any emergency that might arise, we hardly believe they fully understand, or, if they do, it must be for some ulterior motive, for to witness a scene like this would seem to arouse admiration in even the worst.

On May 6th, our necessary speed trials, etc., having been completed, we bade farewell to beautiful little Santa Barbara,

Ruins of a Mission and specimens of California palms, Santa Barbara, Cal.

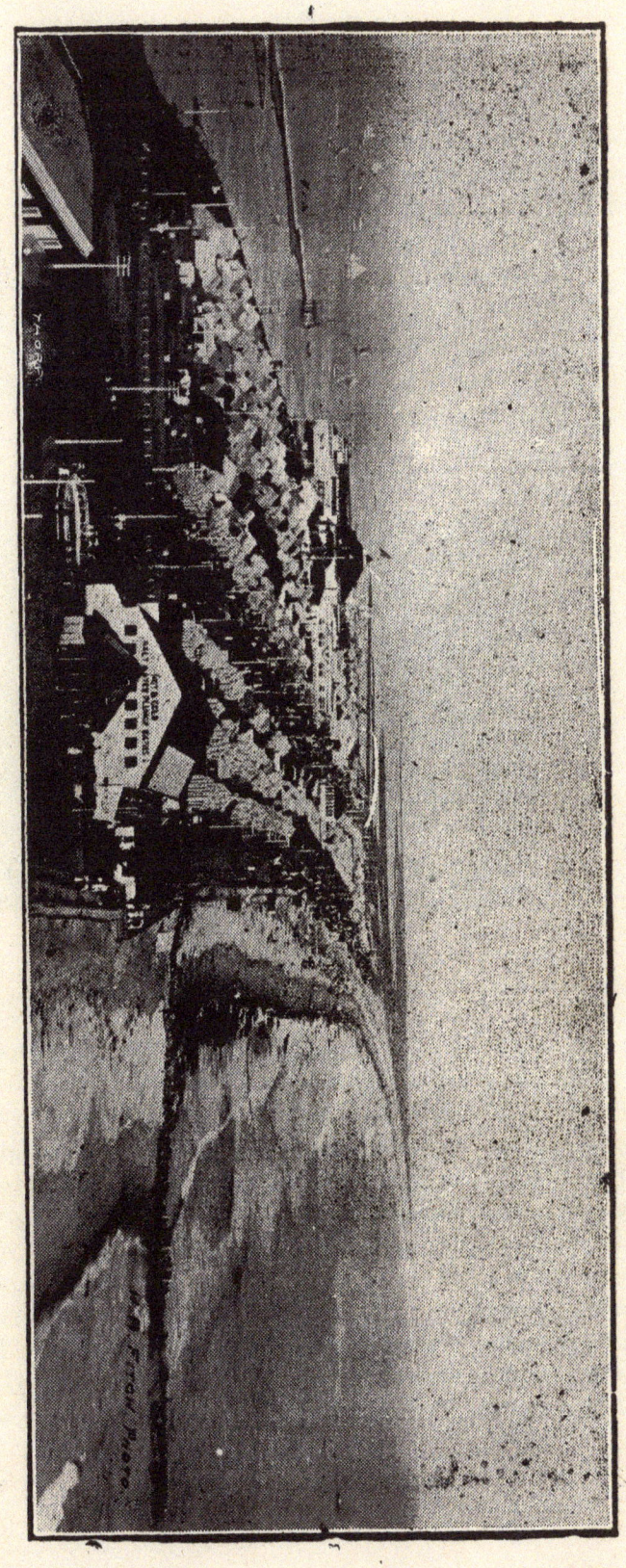

TENT CITY, CORONADO BEACH

In accommodating the pleasure-loving public, the Coronado Beach management has, at great expense, prepared and set aside a portion of its land just between bay and ocean, about half a mile south of the Hotel, as a special resort for summer visitors from the interior and neighboring states, who do not care for hotel life, and yet wish to enjoy the many privileges offered at this attractive resort. Here you may pitch your own tent, or rent one already furnished, and proceed to enjoy a life of ease, comfort and pleasure. ∴ ∴ ∴

with its hospitality, and departed for San Diego, arriving there on the morning of the 7th, and anchoring off the Coronado Hotel, at Coronado Beach.

As Santa Barbara is a beautiful winter resort, so is Coronado, having the large and beautiful hotel of that name located on magnificent grounds, a short distance from the excellent bathing beach. Here indeed is a spot where pessimists and chronic kickers would have to search for a dark spot on the bright and gay life prevalent at Coronado.

HOTEL DEL CORONADO

A short distance from Coronado is the progressive and thoroughly modern little city of San Diego, founded by A. E. Horton in 1867, two years after the Civil war. The population at the present time is estimated to be between 35,000 and 40,000 and appears to be rapidly increasing, large numbers of speculators and miners arriving nearly every day. San Diego is near the Mexican border but is thoroughly American in every respect, possessing all the advantages of our most modern American cities. The city can boast of an excellent traction, fine water, electric lights, the best of schools, one being a large Normal school, and, owing to the excellent climate, has students from all parts of the United States. There is a 1400-acre park; excel-

(Continued on Page 13)

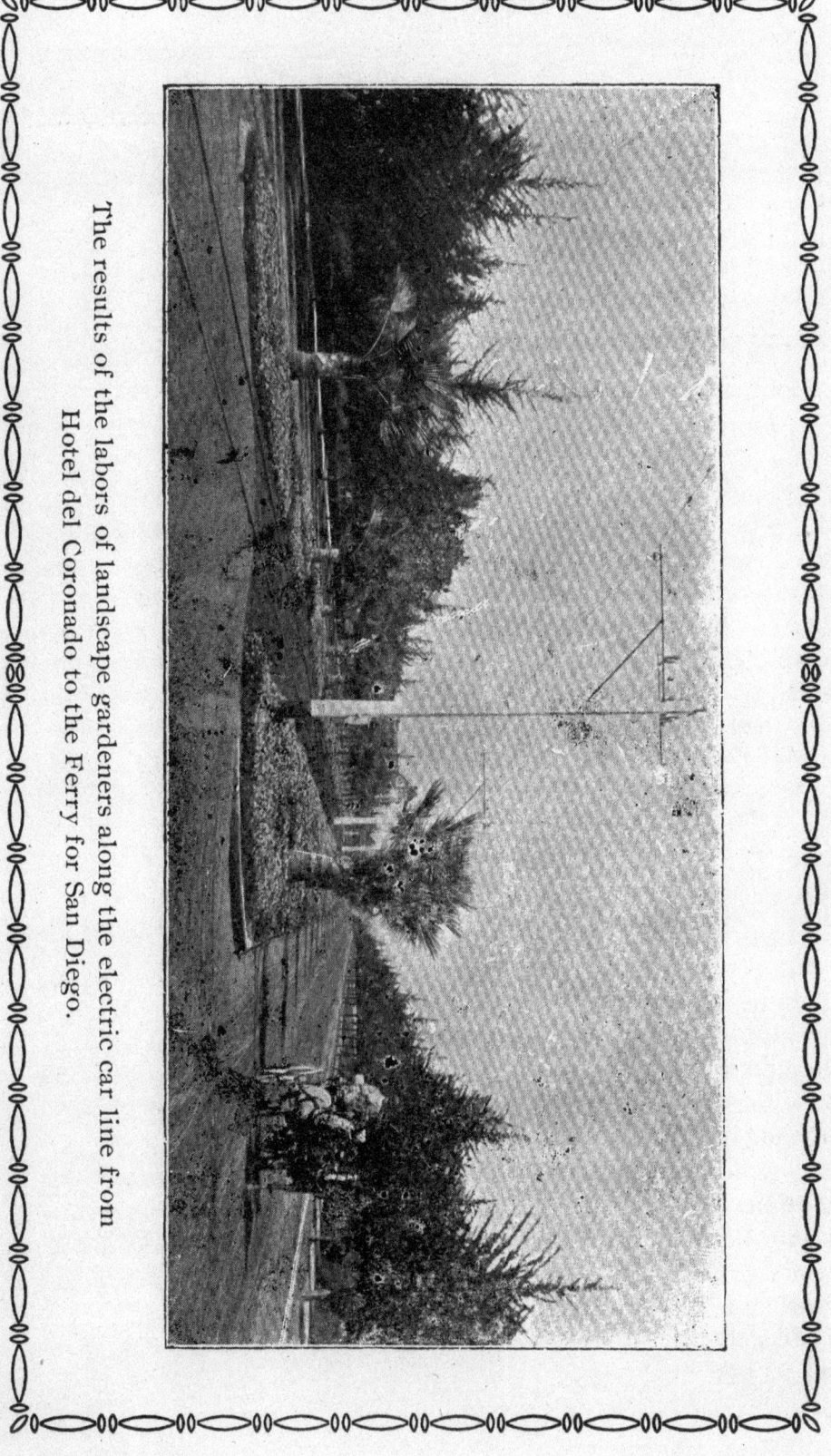

The results of the labors of landscape gardeners along the electric car line from Hotel del Coronado to the Ferry for San Diego.

THE VOLUNTEER

PUBLISHED MONTHLY ON BOARD THE U. S. S. TENNESSEE

CASH, THOMAS & ERWIN, Publishers

Subscription . . . . $1.50 a Year
Single Copies . . . . 15 Cents

Vol. 1   April, 1908.   No. 3

THE TWO TENNESSEES

Though an inland state, Tennessee claims as her sons two of the greatest figures in American Naval annals—Commodore Maury and Admiral Farragut. As Miss Frazier, daughter of the Chief Executive of the Commonwealth of Tennessee broke the bottle of wine upon the prow of the moving vessel and pronounced the words which gave to it the name of Tennessee, a curious historical coincidence came into the consciousness of more than one spectator of the stirring scene. It recalled the contrast between the 14,500 ton warship, with her mighty speed, power, modern guns and armor, and that other Tennessee, the most powerful ironclad built by the Southern Confederacy, the destruction of which was one of the proudest and most brilliant achievements of Farragut.

It was in Mobile Bay, in August, 1864, that the great Tennesseean, passing with his fleet close under the guns of Fort Morgan uttered that famous phrase, "Damn the torpedoes," and led his wooden ships and monitors against Admiral Buchanan's squadron. Here, that formidable ram, the old Tennessee, tried to repeat the tactics of the Merrimac in Hampton Roads, but failed under the terrible onslaught of Farragut's ships.

It is interesting to recall that this old Tennessee, which made such a brave fight in a losing cause, was built at Selma, on the Alabama river, of southern yellow pine and was armed with six-inch iron casemate armor rolled at Atlanta, and this in turn backed by oak sheathing. She carried only six guns, and her engines, taken from a river steamer, only drove her at a speed of from six to eight knots. There were defects in her design, also, which contributed to her undoing, but for all this she was the most formidable floating enemy with which the Union Naval forces had to contend.

In the great battle of Mobile Bay, not a single shot pierced the Tennessee's casemate armor, though the fight was in a narrow channel and at close range—so close that the Confederate ship was rammed repeatedly.

In the forty years which have elapsed since that historic fight, naval construction has been revolutionized, and no more striking illustration of the extent of that revolution can be had than the specifications of these two fighting machines, the old and new Tennessees.

When a modern armored ship can be classed as obsolete after ten years, what term should be applied to an ironclad of 1864 in comparison with an armored cruiser of 1904?

THE PAY BILL

At the time of going to press little action has been taken on the several pay bills before Congress.

The Warren bill was passed by the Senate and appears to have a favorable chance of becoming a law. An amendment was added to this bill providing that it should not increase the pay of any person in the Navy. In phrasing the amendment the purpose intended was over done and the increase will not go to the Marine Corps.

Representative Foss has introduced a bill which equalizes the pay of the Navy and Marine Corps, placing the pay of officers of the Navy on the same basis as officers of the Army and increasing the pay of midshipmen, warrant officers, mates and paymaster's clerks 25 per cent. This bill has been favorably reported by the House.

Enlisted men of the service may rest assured that if any of the bills to increase the pay of the enlisted personnel of the other services succeed in becoming law, the enlisted men of the Navy will receive a fair and liberal increase since the power to raise the pay is vested in the President.

As there still remains several months of legislation, the outlook for a Navy increase seems promising.

THE LAUNCHING OF THE TENNESSEE

The launching of our ship occurred on Saturday morning, December 4, 1904, at 10.50 o'clock. The party, the largest with the exception of the Pennsylvania's launching ever seen at Cramp's, were driven through a hard sleet storm to the ship building yards where the great vessel lay on the ways. Arriving there they were escorted to a platform erected beneath the prow of the vessel. This had been covered with canvas, which was ice coated, but the winter blasts could not chill the enthusiasm of the Tennesseeans who were present for the auspicious occasion. Up to almost the moment the big warship started down the ways a drizzle of sleet and rain fell continuously, but during the actual launching the sun shone through the clouds, considered by the sailors to be a good omen for the future of the ship.

On a small additional platform just beneath the prow of the ship stood Governor and Mrs. Frazier, Miss Keith Frazier, the Sponsor, and her maids—six of those famed southern beauties. In Miss Frazier's hand she held the bottle of Moet & Chandon's champagne, furnished by a Tennessee firm, encased in a welting of gold wire. Finally, just ten minutes before the appointed time, the sound of an axe and then a saw was heard. Then the great ship moved, scarcely, perceptibly, at first. The Sponsor, her face aglow with enthusiasm, struck the bottle of champagne against the bow, and, as if to make sure, struck it again, and said, "I christen thee Tennessee—God speed thee!" At the last launching the Connecticut girl had failed to break the bottle and it had to be done by a seaman. Not so with the Tennessee girl, however. Her aim was true and her arm struck a good blow. The amber fluid bathed the good ship as it glided down into its native element amid the shouts of a now thoroughly enthusiastic crowd.

Following the launch, the invited guests, about 500 in all, were entertained at luncheon in the mould loft.

Governor Frazier's party included the following:

Senator and Mrs. Carmack, General Hanna and mother, General and Mrs. Tysen, General and Mrs. Hardwick, General and Mrs. Pound, General Mountcastle, Colonel and Mrs. Gass, Colonel L. W. Burford, Colonel Caraway, Colonel and Mrs. Milton, Colonel McKellar, Colonel and Mrs. King, Colonel and Mrs.

Abernathy, Colonel and Mrs. Shelton, Colonel and Mrs. Maguire and daughter, Colonel and Mrs. Dibrell, Colonel and Mrs. Harris Brown, Colonel and Mrs. Walter Bell, Colonel and Mrs. Nath Robertson, Colonel and Mrs. Shook, Colonel Martin, Colonel Harvey Alexander, Dr. Ford, Mr. and Mrs. T. B. Carrol, Mr. and Mrs. J. W. Thomas, Mr. and Mrs. A. W. Chambliss, Mr. and Mrs. Percy Warner, Mr. and Mrs. Rutledge Smith, Misses Lorraine Meeks, Estelle Shook, Elizabeth and Martha Thomas, Nell Fall, Viva Harrison, Augusta McKeldin, Mary Guy Trigg, Estelle Bailey, Anna Lee Penn, Louise Baxter, Mary Dibrell.

THE SOCIAL WHIRL

On March 1st, members of the Second Division gave a dinner in the after casemate, port side, gun deck. The bill of fare consisted of turkey and other necessaries, and a delightful time was reported by all present.

On the evening of March 23rd, the date of arrival at Redondo, members of the Chamber of Commerce of that city entertained the crews of the Tennessee, Washington and California at a dance in the pavilion.

A large delegation of bluejackets from each vessel attended and when the Grand March formed at 8.00 p. m., the circle was completely filled. The march was led by Paymaster's Clerk Hunt, of the Tennessee, and Mrs. Matteson, a local woman. The dance consisted of eighteen numbers and two extras, and before the Grand Finale was played, it was well past midnight.

The officers consisted of the members of the Chamber of Commerce.

The ball was thorougly managed and was a decided success from every point of view. Redondo will long be remembered by the Second Division.

Tuesday evening, March 24th, a return ball to the citizens of Redondo was given in the Pavilion, by the crew of the U. S. S. Tennessee.

Beside the civilian attendance, the officers and fifty men from other ships of the Division were invited. The hall was prettily decorated with flags and bunting.

At 8.00 p. m. the Grand March of 500 couples, led by Water Tender Bennett, of the Tennessee, and a San Pedro lady, was formed and places in the line were at a premium. The natty uniforms formed a pretty contrast with the civilian dress and the hall presented a scene of brilliancy and activity.

During intermission, refreshments of ice cream and cake were served.

The hall was filled to the doors, yet through the excellent management and good judgment of the several committees, not the slightest confusion was apparent and much credit is due to the men of the Tennessee who volunteered their services.

The dance order consisted of eighteen thoroughly enjoyable numbers, mainly two-step and waltz, with the Star Spangled Banner as Grand Finale, and it was after midnight before the crowd began to leave.

Following is the order of dances and the several committees:

Grand March ....The Boston Commandery
1. Two-Step ....No Wedding Bells for Me
2. Waltz ....Dreaming
3. Two-Step ....Somewhere
4. Waltz ....I Love You All the Time
5. Two-Step ....Honey Boy
6. Waltz.............When You Know You're Not Forgotten
7. Two-Step ....Mariutch
8. Waltz...School Days
9. Two-Step ....Ida Ho

INTERMISSION

10. Waltz ....Love Me and the World is Mine
11. Two-Step..Napanee
12. Waltz.......................Come the Land of Bohemia
13. Two-Step .... Car Bartick Acid
14. Waltz ....Message of the Violets
15. Two-Step ....I'm Sorry
16. Waltz................................The Merry Widow
17. Two-Step ....The Watermelon Club
18. Waltz........Ev'ry One's in Slumberland but You and Me

The Star Spangled Banner

GOOD NIGHT

Officers and Committees—President, C. A. Reddington, Corp., Secretary, P. Flynn, B. M. 1c; Reception—E. G. Allen, Sergt.; J. W. Holtz, C. M.; J. Wagner, Elect. 1c; Floor—J. B. Bohan, G. M. 1c; F. Krause, B. M. 1c; W. B. Elliott, Oiler; F. Lorenzen, B. M. 1c; Arrangement—G. Austin, C. G. M.; R. A. Young, Elect. 1c; W. T. Bennett, W. T.; F. T. Walling, G. M. 3c; L. M. Bales, C. M.

The Tennessee had the honor of a visit from the champion lady tennis player of the world, Miss May Sutton, of Pasadena, Cal., who lunched on board on the 26th instant.

CRUISING AROUND SOUTHERN CALIFORNIA

(Continued from Page 6)

lent hotels, several large hospitals and sanitariums, and last, but not least, a large and beautiful bay. Point Loma, where is located the largest and most powerful wireless station in the service, is a natural breakwater for San Diego Bay. On the Point there is a large Theosophical Institute; also, the monument recently unveiled in memory of the Bennington dead. Point Loma wireless station is one of the most important in the United States from a naval standpoint, as it is the relay station between the ships at Magdalena Bay and San Francisco, and it is the only means of communication except by boat. On March 14th, while at San Diego, we were joined by the California and South Dakota, the first time the ships which are to comprise the second division of the Pacific Fleet have ever been together, and they presented a very formidable appearance while riding at anchor off Coronado. On the 16th of March, the Tennessee, Washington and California proceeded to San Pedro, Cal., a six-hour run from San Diego, and anchored inside the breakwater, which, by the way, is called the largest in the world. The harbor is well protected, has a good depth of water, and being the sea-port of Los Angeles, seems destined to become a great and thriving shipping port.

The city of San Pedro is of about 8,000 population. It is connected with Los Angeles by an excellent inter-urban car system. Los Angeles, claimed by many as the largest and finest city in California, is located about 18 miles from San Pedro, and the ride on the electric cars is well worth while, since it shows the fertile soil and beauty of Southern California.

The city is now, according to local authorities, nearly 300,000 in population, having more than doubled itself within the past decade. It is beautifully located and contains many points of interest. There are many delightful trips into the suburbs and surrounding cities of Pasadena, Mt. Lowe, Altadena, San Gabriel, etc., all of which are easily accessible by the excellent traction system.

The city interests are well protected by a thoroughly wide awake and up-to-date Chamber of Commerce and no chance for the advancement of Los Angeles is permitted to pass unnoticed, which no doubt accounts much for the marked progression of the city.

During the stay of the Second Division at San Pedro, the Pacific Electric Co. very kindly furnished the enlisted men free transportation over its lines.

The management of Long Beach invited the men of the Division to visit them on March 21st. A number of the places of amusement admitted free all men in uniform, and a great many of the liberty men of the Division enjoyed the hospitality extended.

VISITORS COMING ABOARD AT SAN PEDRO, CAL.

The citizens of San Pedro, Long Beach and Los Angeles seemed unable to do enough to make the men enjoy themselves and the kind treatment and many courtesies extended were very marked.

On March 23rd the ships proceeded to Redondo Beach, a two hour run. On the night of our arrival a ball was given in our honor and on the following evening a return ball was given to the citizens of Redondo, described on another page. Although the stay at this beautiful place lasted but two days it was enjoyed by all. Redondo is a city of about 3,500 population and is a delightful winter resort. It is also a port of Los Angeles. During the stay of the vessels at this port the crews again were given free transportation to Los Angeles and everything possible was done to make the stay a happy one.

The ships left Redondo on the 25th and proceeded to Venice, Cal., rightly styled the Venice of America, for it is indeed a charming place. The same generous hospitality that marked the stay of the vessels at the other ports mentioned was experienced here, the management of the places of amusement admitting all men in uniform free and like San Pedro and Redondo, granting free transportation in any direction on the street cars.

We left Venice on the 27th, and after an over night run, arrived at Monterey, Cal., located about 90 miles south of San Francisco, and one of the prettiest as well as the oldest towns in California. The city is of about 3,500 population, and has a large Army post of 2,000 men.

At 8.15 a. m. March 29th, Admiral Sebree transferred his flag to the California, transferring back again on arrival at San Francisco.

The ships entered the Golden Gate on Sunday afternoon, March 29th, and came to anchor off Folsom street, remaining there until the end of March.

It would be decidedly difficult to select a more interesting cruise than the month spent by the Second Division in southern California, as everything possible was done by the people of the ports visited to make the stay of the ships a thoroughly enjoyable one.

Generous liberty was granted at all points, and in addition large numbers of visitors thronged the ships daily, from 1.30 to 5.00 p. m., which seemed an excellent testimony of the interest of southern Californians in our Navy. It is believed that the cruise has done much to bring the people and the Navy closer together.

Southern California will certainly be pleasantly remembered by the men of the Tennessee.

THE TENNESSEE MINSTREL TROUPE

At San Diego, California, on March 13, the Minstrel Troupe of our ship gave a very pleasing performance before a crowded house at the Garrick Theatre. The amount obtained was donated to the Navy Relief Society fund for the benefit of the wives and children of deceased officers and men. The sum of $516 was realized after paying expenses.

The San Diego Union of the 15th contained the following account of the performance:

SAILORS MINSTREL PROVES CLEVER PERFORMANCE

New and Witty Gags, Catchy Songs and Appreciative Audience Are Striking Features

Before an audience which crowded the Garrick theatre to the very doors, the sailors of the U. S. S. Tennessee gave a minstrel show last night which would have done credit to any traveling troupe on the road.

Appropriate costumes, new and witty gags, good voices, and an appreciative audience were features very much in evidence. While almost every crack of the end men, of which there were six, H. R. Renner, J. Meegan, E. M. Mounts, S. Weinstein, J. Thomas and G. Cohen was liberally applauded, songs and references to Admiral Sebree, who was an interested spectator from one of the boxes, were received with especial favor, never failing to bring down the house. Several good hits with a local reference were also made.

The first part of the performance last night which was given throughout in regular minstrel style was devoted to songs and jokes. Among the former an end song by H. R. Renner entitled "Dixie Dan," one by E. M. Mounts entitled "Somebody Lied" and a march song by F. T. Walling "My Yankee Sailor Boy," all supported by full chorus, were especially catchy.

The olio gave chance for a number of comedy skits and unique vaudeville stunts, all good, and the program closed with a one-act farce entitled "Dutch Justice," which for brightness was far ahead of any playlette of it's character seen here in some time.

The olio included the following numbers: Thomas and Pettibone, "A Little Bit of Nonsense;" the Tennessee Musical club; Aschauer and Wirth, "The Jew and Hamolet;" The Tennessee Acrobatic Troupe; Ward, Pettibone and Renner, "Here, There and Everywhere;" Eagan and Pritchard, in a comedy skit, "Is He In;" The Golden Gate Quartette, W. Elliott, F. T. Walling, H. R. Renner and J. O. Johnson.

The complete program was as follows: Interlocuter, F. T. Walling; Tambos, H. R. Renner, E. M. Mounts, J. Thomas; Bones, J. H. Meegan, S. Weinstein, G. Cohen; Circle, A. Wrightson, A. A. Achauer, J. T. Ward, W. Elliot, M. Wolfertz, A. Quattle, J. Egan, E. Pritchard, J. O. Johnson, J. E. Persing, W. Kelly, T. F. Calhoun, A. H. Pettibone, J. V. Madison.

PART I.

1. Opening Chorus—"Sing Me a Song of the South"..Company
2. "Hail to Admiral Sebree".........................Company
3. "Here Come Our End Men".........................Company
4. Comic Song—"I'm Afraid to Come Home"....... G. Cohen
5. Solo—"When Sweet Marie Was Sweet Sixteen" M.W. Kelly
6. End Song—"Somebody Lied"............... E. M. Mounts
7. Solo—"Won't You Waltz Home Sweet Home" T. F. Calhoun
8. End Song—"I've Got to See De Minstrel Show" J. H. Meegan
9. Solo—"Just to Remind You".....................W. Elliot
10. End Song—"Dixie Dan".................... H. R. Renner
11. March Song—"My Yankee Sailor Boy"...... F. T. Walling

Grand Finale—"The Yankee Sailor Boy"

INTERMISSION.

PART II—OLIO.

1. Thomas & Pettibone..............A Little Bit of Nonsense
2. The Tennessee Musical Club ....
3. Aschauer & Wirth.............The Jew and the Ham-o-let
4. The Tennessee Acrobatic Troupe ....
5. Ward, Pettibone & Renner....Here, There and Everywhere
6. Egan & Pritchard, in a Comedy Skit..............Is He In
7. The Golden Gate Quartette........................
    W. Elliot, F. T. Walling, H. R. Renner, J. O. Johnson
8. A One-Act Farce, entitled...................Dutch Justice

On March 26th, another show was given to a fair sized audience in the Venice Auditorium at Venice, Cal., for the benefit of the same society and an additional sum of $37 was realized.

GRAPE PICKING IN SOUTHERN CALIFORNIA

IN THE SWIM

APOLOGIES TO MAUD MULLER

A seaman on a sunny day
Was tarring down the forward stay.

An ink slinger out for a walk
Stopped to have a little talk.

He murmured without e'en a frown
What are you doing, tarring down?

No, said the seaman, somewhat slow,
I'm in Alaska shoveling snow.

The quill pusher then turned his neck
And ambled briskly down the deck.

The seaman to a rook then said,
A yeoman for a leather head.

Some of the strong pulls fade away when it comes to hoisting the dinghy.

Division Officer to Rookie—Guide right. Rookie—Aye, aye, sir; been guyed right and left.

Why didn't they change the uniform in Adam's time; it would have been a re-leaf then.

Strange it seems that when the tongue is thick the excuse for staying over time is too thin.

In calling Dam Li, the laundryman in a First Division ship, by name, remember Li in Chinese is pronounced Lee.

The mess-boy argued—His name am not Jones, it am Joans. I sees, said the other, you puts de access on de pronoun.

How long was Washington dead when President Roosevelt was inaugurated? I dun no, but it ain't been dead since.

Barber, barber, shave a pig, said a First Division kid,
I'll shave you soon was Ambler's dig, and pretty soon he did.

Officer-of-the-Deck to Overtimer—You were told to be back at a quarter of twelve; here it is 3. Overtimer—Aye, Aye, sir, a quarter of twelve is 3.

This time it is the Scat (Arkansas) Blade that publishes a letter rit by a boy on the Tennessee and the Blade says that since Ez left Scat they have learnt things about the Navy. Ez says that he sets at the table side o' Molly Coddle—if they haint got wimen in the Navy what is Molly Coddle doing thar. 'Tis time for Scat young men to foller Ez's footsteps, for tiz a shame when wimen have to fight.

AN EPITAPH FOR A HOSPITAL APPRENTICE.

Willie's gone, the dear kid, we ne'er shall see him more,
He thought he drank of H_2O—'twas H_2SO_4.

If that 8-minute parting kiss becomes a fad, how will we ever get away for the Philippines.

The connecting link between the animal and vegetable kingdom seems to be canned willie hash.

Our fleet's journey is near an end—now where next will it go;
A lime-juice fireman remarked, 'Evans only knows.

AT SAN DIEGO

Will you have a lobster, M——an said.
This is so sudden, quoth the maid.

The laundryman of the Tennessee, breaking into the ball room: See yar, come straight back, de gent am dun cum for his shirt.

Kelly, the baseball player, says a chicken farm for his next cruise—perhaps he is going to feed some of the flies he caught to the chicks.

The Heave: What is the most dangerous nation? The End Man: Don't Know. The Heave: Vacci-nation. Cause it is always up in arms.

At the Long Beach Ball—She: Beg pardon, your name please. Wize acres from the third division: William Arrimee. She: This is so sudden.

Bashful "Heave" at the Ball: What must I tell her when I see her home, Good evening, or Good night. 3rd Cruise: Neither—Good morning.

Charlie is coaxing the hair faithfully with a preparation labeled "Guaranteed to help when everything else fails." 'Tis the fifth bottle, but Charlie says he has not tried everything else yet.

Out in Podunk—I say, Maria, Frank writes home about docking a Navy greyhound. Maria—Don't read such cruel things to me; there ought to be a law against cutting off them dog's tails.

John N., who has been laboriously raising a mustache, is anxious to know what color it will be when full grown. The Volunteer predicts, at the rate it is coming along, that it may be gray.

Though money and brains are a beautiful pair,
It is very consoling to see there
Are one or two guys in the messman branch
Who "Make out" with but little of either.

RIFLE MATCH.

A Rifle team from the Tennessee contested with the Southern California Rifles at Redondo on March 24th. Although the ship's team made an excellent showing, they lost by a score of 1102 against 1155 for the shore team. The showing of the team is considered marvelous, as the members of the shore team constituted some experts, while the only practice that the ship's team had previous to the match was with the the sub-target machine on board ship.

Surgeon Guest of the Tennessee made the highest score for his team and sixth highest of the day.

Captain Howard umpired the match and Paymaster Venable and Ensign Holmes acted as score keepers. Sergeant Allen was marker.

The following is the score of the match by totals:

Southern Cal. Rifles	200 yds. Offhand	300 yds. Sitting	300 yds. Prone	Individual totals
Neff, 30-40 Win. Mil	42	45	41	128
Weddington, 33 Win. Rep	42	41	41	124
Wolf, 30-30 Win. Rep	41	40	41	122
Simpson, 25-20 Win. Rep	39	39	42	120
Ostrander, 303 Savage	40	43	35	118
Andrews, 25-35 Win. Rep	36	38	37	111
Dr. Alden, 45-70 Springfield	37	34	39	110
Watts, 25-35 Win. Rep	31	42	36	109
Orrill, 32 Win. Special	35	35	39	109
Chandler, 32 Win. Special	34	37	35	106
	377	394	386	1,157

Tennessee Team (Krags)				
Surgeon Guest	36	42	39	117
Hamric	40	39	37	116
Smith	36	39	41	116
Bales	38	39	39	116
Williams	37	37	39	113
Car. Meade	36	37	39	112
Hellriegel	36	33	38	107
Lieut. Meyer	36	35	35	106
Hartson	29	36	35	100
Graichairm	34	31	34	99
	358	368	376	1,102

LOG FOR MARCH, 1908

Sunday, 1—Dropped anchor at Santa Barbara, Cal., at 3.07 p. m ; distance from San Francisco, 287 miles.

Monday, 2—At 9.35 a. m. got underway and stood out from anchorage for tactical data; exercised at man overboard; anchored in anchorage at 12.46 p. m.

Tuesday, March 3—At 8.30 a. m. got underway and stood ont into channel for tactical data, speeds varying from 10 to 18 knots; at 12.38 p. m. anchored in anchorage off city.

Wednesday, 4—Got underway at 9.00 a. m.; completed trial runs over measured mile at 20, 12½ and 8 knots; at 4.26 p. m. anchored off city.

Thursday, 5—Sent baseball team ashore to play local team.

Friday, 6—Got underway at 5.54 p. m. for San Diego, Cal.

Saturday, 7—At 7.35 a. m. anchored off Coronado Beach, San Diego, Cal.; the Mayor and committee of San Diego called upon the Commander, Second Division, Pacific Fleet.

Sunday, 8, San Diego—Paul Majocchi, seaman, was transferred to the Marine ward, St. Joseph's hospital, San Diego, injured eye; Commanding Officer Fort Rosecrans called officially on the Commander, Second Division; tug Fortune got underway and stood into the harbor; the Commander Second Division, and Commanding Officer called officially upon the Commanding Officer of Fort Rosecrans; tug Fortune stood out of harbor to the southward.

Monday, 9, San Diego—Painting ship; sent baseball party and track team ashore.

Tuesday, 10, San Diego—Albany stood into inner harbor and anchored at 4.00 p. m., fired a salute of 13 guns and was answered with 7 guns; continued painting ship.

Wednesday, 11, San Diego—Continued painting ship; visitors received on board; exercised at search light drill.

Thursday, 12, San Diego—Called away all boats and exercised under oars during morning; sent minstrel troupe to San Diego for rehearsal; R. C. Swanson and W. Samuels enlisted on board this vessel as coal passers; Commander Second Division held reception on board from 3 to 5 p. m.

Friday, 13, San Diego—The South Dakota stood in and anchored at 10.35 a. m.; Commanding Officer South Dakota called officially on the Commander Second Division; sent baseball party and Minstrel troupe ashore, and Minstrel troupe gave show that evening at the Garrick theatre.

Saturday, 14, San Diego—The Commanding Officer of California called officially on the Commander Second Division; the Commander Second Division, the Commanding Officer and Flag Lieutenant called officially upon the Commanding Officer South Dakota; E. D. Park enlisted on board this vessel as a coal passer.

Sunday, 15, San Diego—The Ward-room officers of the South Dakota called on the Commander Second Division, Commanding Officer and Ward-room officers.

Monday, 16—The Buffalo stood into San Diego harbor and fired a salute of 13 guns; division, except South Dakota, got underway at 10.00 a. m. for San Pedro, Cal., and anchored there at 6.03 p. m.

Tuesday, 17, San Pedro, Cal.—Committee representing Chamber of Commerce, Los Angeles and Long Beach, called upon the Division Commander.

Wednesday, 18, San Pedro—Visitors came on board from San Pedro and Long Beach; made preparations for coaling.

Thursday, 19, San Pedro—All hands engaged in coaling ship; Collier Justin shoved off at 6.50 p. m.

Friday, 20, San Pedro—Commanding Officer and party left ship to inspect site for small arms target practice.

Saturday, 21, San Pedro—Cleaning ship; Division Commander called officially upon the Commanding Officer of California.

Sunday, 22, San Pedro—Commanding Officer California called officially upon the Commanding Officer Tennessee; sent rifle team and baseball party ashore.

Monday, 23—Got underway 10.25 a. m. for Redondo Beach, and anchored off town at 12.35 p. m.; sent rifle team ashore to participate in rifle match; sent party ashore to attend ball given by citizens of Redondo.

Tuesday, 24, Redondo Beach—Sent liberty party ashore and party to attend ball Redondo Pavilion, given by the crew.

Wednesday, 25—At 9.53 a. m. got underway and steamed for Venice, Cal., anchoring off town at 11.02 a. m.; salute of 13 guns was fired on shore and was answered gun for gun by this ship.

Thursday, 26, Venice, Cal.—Crew engaged in routine drills; rough sea; used oil from hawse pipe; gave minstrel show ashore.

Friday, 27, Venice—At 9.56 a. m. got underway for Monterey, Cal.; sighted the Albany standing into Santa Barbara.

Saturday, 28, Monterey, Cal.—At 9.55 a. m. anchored off Monterey; Commanding Officer of Army Post called officially upon the Division Commander.

Sunday, 29—Division Commander left the ship at 8.15 a. m. and transferred his flag to the California; 9.00 a. m. got underway for San Francisco and anchored in harbor at 4.33 p. m.; Division Commander returned on board at 5.00 p. m. and hoisted his flag.

Monday, 30, San Francisco—Charleston fired salute at 8 a. m. of 13 guns, was answered by this ship with 7; Yorktown steamed out of harbor for Mare Island; Chief Master-at-Arms P. B. Golden transferred; Chief Master-at-Arms J. M. Acuff reported on board for duty.

Tuesday, 31, San Francisco—Had exercise at landing force; Commanding Officers of Tennessee, Washington and California called officially upon the Division Commander.

Army & Navy Union

A branch garrison, No. 110, of the Army & Navy Union has been organized on board and now has 38 members. The following are the officers of the organization: Commander, J. J. Bennett; Vice-Commander, C. E. Lawrence; Adjutant, W. A. Speck; Junior Vice-Commander, R. C. Saline; Paymaster, C. Ambler; Officer of the Watch, C. King; Officer of the Day, T. F. Calhoun. All men desiring to join are cordially invited to see Water Tender J. J. Bennett. It is hoped to make this garrison one of the largest afloat.

Boxing at San Pedro

Before the San Pedro Athletic Club, on Friday, March 20th, the following boxing contests took place:

L. Frommer, Tennessee, vs. Kid Mahlor, of San Pedro; six rounds; decision awarded to Frommer.

J. J McDonald, Tennessee, vs. Jimmy Lee, of Watts; six rounds; no decision.

Spike Higgins, of California, vs. Abdul the Turk, of Los Angeles; no decision.

Referee: Reporter of San Pedro News.

The bouts were clean and snappy, the concensus of opinion being that the bluejackets had slightly the best of the second and third contests, although no decisions were awarded in the matches, except the first, which was won on a knockout.

Baseball Scores of the Past Month

The baseball team, while not having been able to win a majority of the games during the month have made a very creditable showing, considering the fact that the teams played were in nearly every instance either professionals or semi-professionals. The following is a summary of games during March: At Santa Barbara—Tennessee, 3, Portland, 9; at San Diego—Tennessee, 3, San Diego, 4; at San Pedro—Tennessee, 3, U. S. S. California, 5; Tennessee, 0, Merchants, 8; Tennessee, 4, Gerdue, 10; at Redondo, Tennessee, 14, Redoneo, 10.

Novelty Knives and Razors
Any name, ship, photo or emblem you desire on handles
Prices from 80 cents up   Goods guaranteed
Albert E. Auger, Engineer's Storeroom

Rubber Stencils Made
Ditty box locks for sale   Keys of all kinds made to order
H. Kohlman, Shipwright, Carpenter Shop

Itinerary—U. S. S. Tennessee

Port	Arrival	Departure	Miles
League Island, Pa. (com's'd)	July 17, '06	Nov. 1, '06	233
Hampton Roads, Va	Nov. 3 "	" 8 "	98
Piney Point, Md	" 8 "	" 8 "	1834
Colon, Panama	" 14 "	" 15 "	130
Chiriqui Lagoon	" 16 "	" 16 "	1041
Ponce, Porto Rico	" 21 "	" 22 "	1285
Hampton Roads, Va	" 26 "	Dec. 16 "	240
League Island, Pa	Dec. 18 "	Apr. 12, '07	233
Hampton Roads, Va	Apr. 13 '07	" 14 "	15
Lynn Haven Bay, Va	" 14 "	" 16 "	16
Hampton Roads, Va	" 16 "	May 16 "	530
Provincetown, Mass	May 18 "	" 24 "	53
Boston, Mass	" 25 "	June 5 "	555
Hampton Roads, Va	June 7 "	" 11 "	382
Newport, R. I	" 12 "	" 14 "	3112
Royan, France	" 23 "	July 2 "	52
Ile D' Aix, France	July 2 "	" 3 "	10
La Rochelle, France	" 3 "	" 11 "	235
Brest, France	" 12 "	" 25 "	3194
Tompkinsville, S. I	Aug. 6 "	Aug. 16 "	270
Hampton Roads, Va	" 17 "	" 17 "	392
Newport, R. I	" 18 "	" 19 "	265
Boston, Mass	" 20 "	Sept. 30 "	265
Newport, R. I	Oct. 1 "	Oct. 4 "	392
Hampton Roads, Va	" 5 "	" 12 "	1904
Port of Spain, Trinidad	" 18 "	" 24 "	3300
Rio de Janeiro, Brazil	Nov. 4 "	Nov. 10 "	1044
Montevideo, Uruguay	" 13 "	" 19 "	1325
Punta Arenas, Chile	" 23 "	" 27 "	2760
Callao, Peru	Dec. 5 "	Dec. 12 "	2240
Acapulco, Mexico	" 19 "	" 22 "	785
Pichilinque Bay, Mexico	" 25 "	" 28 "	315
Magdalena Bay, Mexico	" 29 "	Feb. 15 "	1026
San Francisco, Cal	Feb. 20 "	" 29 "	287
Santa Barbara, Cal	Mar. 1 "	Mar. 6 "	164
San Diego, Cal	" 6 "	" 16 "	96
San Pedro, Cal	" 16 "	" 23 "	18
Redondo, Cal	" 23 "	" 25 "	9
Venice, Cal	" 25 "	" 27 "	275
Monterey, Cal	" 28 "	" 29 "	92
San Francisco, Cal	" 29 "		

When You Buy A Pen,
Get
The Pen that Inks the Point

The Parker Pen!

The Kind That Has The

Lucky Curve

J. J. Bennett, Water Tender
Exclusive Agent
Aboard this Ship

The Saturday Evening Post

A clean, thoroughly up-to-date weekly :: Brimfull of bright news and good stories

CLOWRY
Quartermaster
Has Them All

What You Do Not See
ASK FOR

Cosmopolitan
Motor
Metropolitan
Pearson's
Ainslee's
Argosy
Broadway
Burr McIntosh
Collier's Weekly
Everybody's
Judge
Leslie's Weekly
Life
Outing
Review of Reviews
Scientific American
Scrap Book
Smart Set
Success
Sunset
Travel Magazine
World's Work
Our Navy
Red Book
Blue Book
Popular
Harmsworth
   Self Educator

BOOK FIVE

THE VOLUNTEER

MAY, 1908

U. S. S. TENNESSEE

PUBLISHED MONTHLY

$ We Save You $
Best Investment *at the* Navy Yard

¶ We have for sale some of the best and cheapest lots in Bremerton and Charleston, Washington, near the Navy Yard gate. If city lots are preferred we are the exclusive agents for the *National Land and Investment Company*, and can sell you lots and acreage cheaper than any other Real Estate Agent in the State.

¶ Our suburban lots in Tacoma are the most beautiful residential locations in that city, and the best suburban investment in the Northwest. No matter where you are located you can purchase from us with perfect safety. We have sold lots of property to boys scattered throughout the different squadrons and will refer you to them at any time.

Our terms are $25.00 down and $5.00 or more per month until paid up in full.

Lehmann & Poindexter

Bankers and Real Estate

Offices: Charleston and Bremerton, Wash.

We pay 4 per cent on time deposits.

NAVY RELIEF SOCIETY

ADMIRAL OF THE NAVY, GEORGE DEWEY,
President

Mrs. R. B. Bradford	First Vice-Pres.
Mrs. A. S. Barker	Second Vice-Pres.
Mrs. R. T. Mulligan	Third Vice-Pres.
Mrs. B. H. Buckingham	Rec. Secty.
Mrs. C. H. Davis	Cor. Secty.
Mr. E. T. Stotesbury	Treas.
Paymr. Gen. A. S. Kenny (Ret.),	Asst. Treas.
Mr. J. G. Johnson }	
Mr. J. K. McCammon }	Counsel

Washington, D C., March 30, 1908

Dear Sir:

The Board of Managers of the Navy Relief Society are greatly indebted to you, your officers and men, and the TENNESSEE Minstrels for their generous check just received.

As the expenditures for last year were greater than the receipts an effort has been made to interest the service at large in this good work which is so distinctly our own, and we are all greatly encouraged by the fine and early support the TENNESSEE has given us.

Trusting the spirit shown by your good ship may indicate the spirit of all, I remain,

Very truly yours,

(*Signed*) GEORGE DEWEY,
Admiral of the Navy,
Pres. Navy Relief Society

CAPTAIN T. B. HOWARD,
U. S. S. Tennessee.

CAPTAIN THOMAS B. HOWARD
U. S. Navy
Commanding U. S. S. Tennessee

THE VOLUNTEER

Vol. 1   May, 1908   No. 4

CRUISING THROUGH WASHINGTON

On April 1, 1908, a few seconds after the signal "get underway" went up on the afteryard of the Tennessee, the Second Division of the Pacific Fleet, consisting of the U. S. S. Tennessee (flagship), Washington and California, left the Folsom Street anchorage in San Francisco Harbor, stood out in natural order through the historic Golden Gate and headed into the bracing air and turbulent sea of the great Northwest.

The cruise up the Coast, though a little choppy, was delightful in other respects, the vessels steaming closely to the scenic shores of the North Pacific during the entire voyage. It was almost an uneventful cruise, with perhaps a passing sail or a salute from some lighthouse, until April 4th, when Tatoosh island was picked up and the Division rounded Cape Flattery, stood into the Straits of Juan de Fuca and dropped anchor at Port Angeles, in the State of Washington.

Before attempting to describe the month spent in the grand State of Washington it would perhaps be well to look into the history of the land.

Washington, called the Evergreen State, though a few years ago practically unknown to the people throughout the United States, has bounded forward almost within a decade. It is located in the extreme northwestern part of the United States, bounded on the north by the Straits of Juan de Fuca and British Columbia, on the east by Idaho, on the south by Oregon and on the west by the Pacific Ocean. The State has an area of 69,180 square miles, and has a natural division in the Cascade Mountains which cross the entire State, three-fifths of the land being on the east side and two-fifths on the west, known respectively as Eastern and Western Washington.

The scenic beauties of the State are almost beyond description. The snow-capped peaks, the beautiful lakes, the waters of Puget Sound, etc., have no doubt furnished inspiration to a great many artists in recent years. Among the high mountains in Western Washington are Rainier or Tacoma Mountain, 14,536 feet; Baker, 11,100 feet; Adams, 12,470 feet. In the Olympic Range near the Pacific Coast we have Mount Olympus, 8,130 feet and Mount Fitzhenry, 8,098 feet.

The principal river is the Columbia, 425 miles long, separating Washington from Oregon and emptying into the Pacific Ocean. Besides the Columbia there are eleven other rivers of more or less importance which flow into Puget Sound from the Cascade Mountains.

Washington contains a number of lakes noted for their beauty. The largest is Lake Chelan, fifty miles long, one to three miles wide, and greatest depth of 1,500 feet. This lake extends from the Columbia River into the heart of the mountains, and it is here that the tourist can enjoy the coveted pleasure of sailing for thirty miles through the high snow-covered peaks from seven to ten thousand feet high. The scenery here is not surpassed even in the historic Alps.

There are really no good sea ports on the Pacific Coast of the State, with perhaps the exception of Willapa and Gray's Harbor, but Puget Sound contains many delightful places from the Straits of Juan de Fuca to Olympia, a distance of 200 miles. The waters of the Sound vary in depth from 60 to 1,000 feet, with a tide of from 9 to 18 feet.

A few of the things of which Washington can boast follow: The best wheat land in the world, with an annual production of over thirty million bushels; an excellent fruit country; 441 shingle mills and 419 lumber mills, with an annual output valued at $35,000,000; forty-five salmon canneries, employing ten thousand people and producing goods annually, valued at $8,000,000. There are also twenty-three coal mines in operation in Puget Sound Basin and the Cascade Mountains.

Washington contains fifty-nine places of over one thousand population, twenty-eight over two thousand, nine over five thousand and five of twenty thousand and upward.

The first records we have in history of this State was the discovery of the Straits of Juan de Fuca by a Greek pilot of that name, then in the service of the Mexican Government. It is claimed that in 1175 a Spanish navigator, Bruno Heceta, sailed along the Coast and discovered the Columbia River, but did not enter. In 1792 Captain Robert Gray, a New England navigator, sailed up the North Pacific Coast, discovered the mouth of the Columbia River, entered and explored for fifteen miles, giving the river the name of his vessel, the "Columbia." It was this discovery that gave the

United States the strongest claim to this land, known as the Oregon country and drained by the Columbia. Captain G. Vancouver explored the waters of Puget Sound the same year.

The first military expedition sent out was known as the Lewis and Clark expedition, in 1805 and 1806, under President Jefferson's administration. This expedition crossed the Mississippi, explored to the mouth of the Columbia and camped there during the winter. The second expedition was sent out under Captain J. C. Fremont and reached Vancouver. A naval expedition under Captain Wilkes explored the waters of Puget Sound in 1841, and the first settlement was made in Eastern Washington by the Northwestern Fur Company in 1870.

The ownership north of the Columbia River was claimed by Great Britain and the United States until 1846, when by treaty the former took all land north of the forty-ninth parallel and the latter all land south, except the end of Vancouver Island. Dispute again arose over the boundaries in 1859 and was not settled until 1872, when, by arbitration, the German Emperor decided in favor of the United States.

On August 14, 1848, the land north of the Columbia was organized into the Territory of Washington and south into the Territory of Oregon. Gold was discovered about this time and a large increase in population began to flow in and intrude on the Indians' hunting-grounds, which led to the Indian wars of 1855-56-57.

On November 11, 1889, Washington was admitted to the Union as a State, and though not far advanced at that time, is today one of the grandest and strongest commonwealths of which the United States is made.

Returning to our cruise, we find the Second Division, at daybreak, in the pretty little harbor of Port Angeles. Here is one of the quaintest and most reserved places in the State. The population numbers about 2,800. Owing to the mountain range close behind the town the railroads are unable to reach Port Angeles, or at least the expense attached has kept any road from making an attempt. However, at the present time there is a company buying up land with a view to completing the road to Port Townsend, where connections with other railroads and transportation lines may be had. The present means of communication is by boats which touch points in Puget Sound and the Straits, reaching Port Angeles bi-weekly. There is a salmon cannery at Port Angeles which furnishes work for a large number of the residents. The harbor is well protected by a natural breakwater in Ediz Hook, and has a good depth of water. It is especially important, as it is the first port for anchorage of vessels arriving in Juan de Fuca Straits from the Pacific. The ships were opened to visitors and a large number of citizens availed themselves of an opportunity to visit the largest vessels that have ever visited their city.

On April 6th we proceeded to Port Townsend, in Admiralty Inlet, at the entrance to the waters of Puget Sound, arriving there about 1 p. m., a distance of thirty-seven miles. On arrival at Port Townsend the members of the Chamber of Commerce came on board and welcomed the Division Commander and the Commanding Officers of the vessel to their city.

Port Townsend, according to the census, has a population of 5,300, but it is claimed by local authorities that the city has over 8,000 people. Fort Worden is located there and has a garrison of 1,000 men. The city is up-to-date and progressive, an excellent testimonial to this fact being the activity in real estate speculation. The citizens of Port Townsend came off to visit the vessels in large numbers, and it is safe to say that nearly every one who was able visited the Washington, named after their State.

After two days' stay at Port Townsend, on April 8th, at 9 a. m., the Tennessee and California got underway for Bellingham, the Washington proceeding to Seattle. Arriving at Bellingham about 1 p. m., as soon as the anchors had been dropped, the Chamber of Commerce boarded the flagship, and through Mr. T. G. Newman, spokesman for Mayor de Mattos, welcomed the officers and men to the city of Bellingham.

Bellingham, formerly called Whatcom, is located on Bellingham Bay, in Whatcom County, and is about seventy-nine miles north of Seattle. The city has a population of about 26,000 and is thoroughly up-to-date. The Great Northern, Northern Pacific, and Bellingham Bay and British Columbia railroads run through the city, which, with excellent boat service, gives Bellingham the best transportation facilities of any of the cities in that section. Lake Whatcom, four miles distant, is a delightful place and also the source of the city's water supply, it being obtained from there by the gravity system. It has excellent car service and schools, the State Normal School being located here. In December, 1890, Whatcom and Sehome were consolidated and called New Whatcom; in 1901 the name was again changed to Whatcom, and in 1903 to Bellingham.

During the stay at Bellingham the citizens did everything possible to entertain both officers and men. A dance was given in honor of the visit, which is fully described on another page. Baseball teams from the two ships played with the local teams, and on April 10th the Tennessee's band gave a concert in the Fairyland Skating Rink.

Believing that the bluejackets should have some fitting souvenir, the Young Men's Commercial Club ordered 2,000 shingles from the largest shingle mill in the world, around which were wrapped 2,000 canned salmon wrappers from the

(Continued on Page 10)

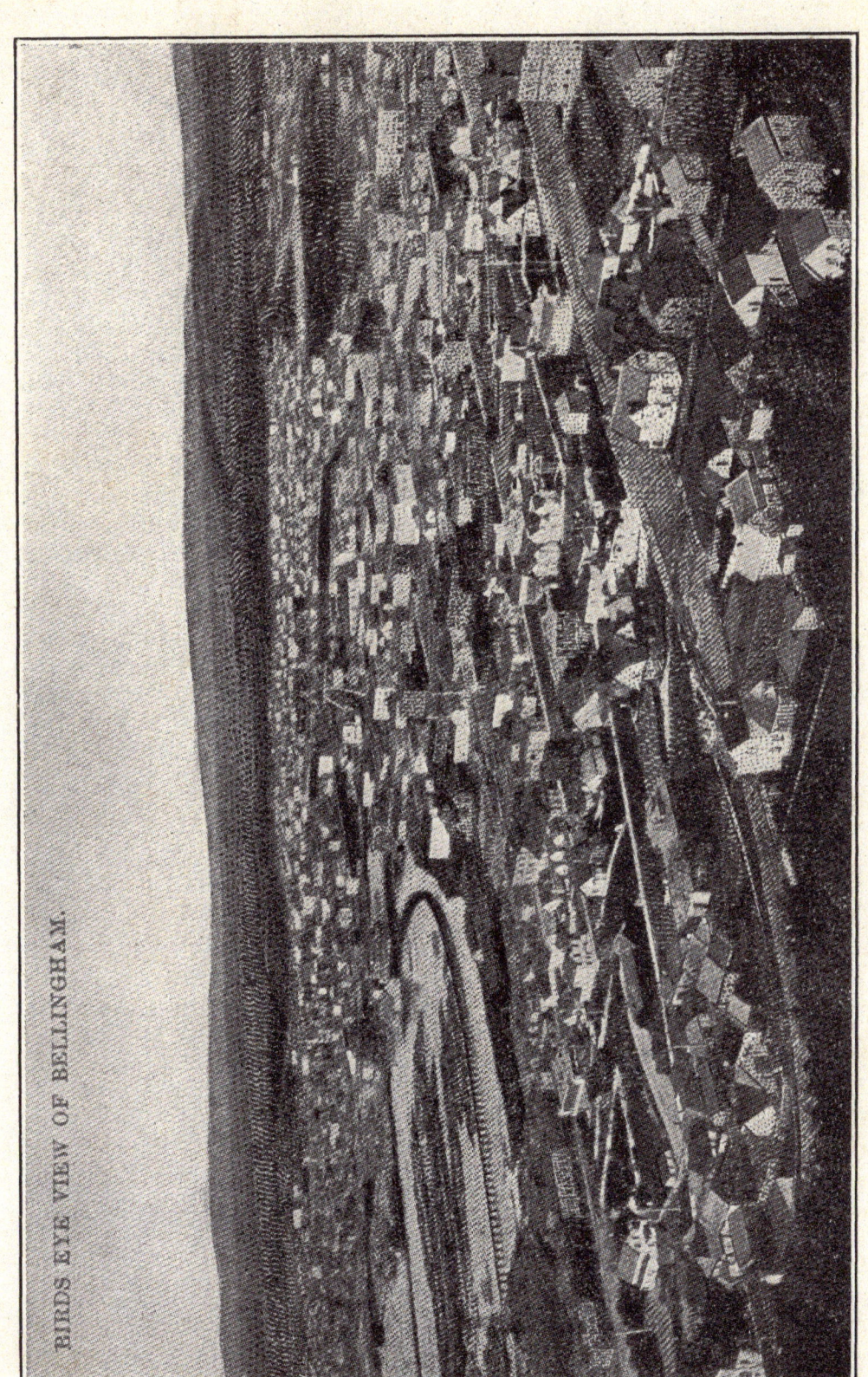
BIRDS EYE VIEW OF BELLINGHAM.

THE VOLUNTEER

PUBLISHED MONTHLY ON BOARD THE U. S. S. TENNESSEE

CASH, THOMAS & IRWIN, Publishers.

Subscription...$1.50 a Year
Single Copies..15 Cents

Vol. 1   May, 1908   No. 4

OUR UNIFORM

Since the large number of visitors received on board during the month of April have nearly all asked questions in regard to the meaning of different parts of the uniform, we publish, for the information of those who were unable to answer, the following:

"With the exception of the stars on the collar the suit is copied from the English. In the early days of the British Navy it was the custom to wear the hair in a queue and keep it greased, which naturally ruined the neck of the blouse. This added the wide collar of the same material, but was later changed to a more endurable material of blue drill, which lasted until the queue vanished, when it was again restored to the former material—that of the navy-blue blouse. At first the neck was exposed, but in later years thoughtfulness regarding the welfare of the men added the neck-piece. The rows of braid on the sleeve, used in our Navy to represent seamen, ordinary and apprentice seamen, formerly represented in the British service England and Ireland, the two top rows being joined and the bottom row separated from the others representing Scotland, which had not joined at that time. The rows of braid on the collar represent Nelson's victories of Aboukir, Copenhagen and Trafalgar, the last battle resulting in his death which caused such intense mourning that the black neckerchief was added. The wide trousers were made for convenience in landing in the surf, in order that the pant legs might be easily and quickly rolled up."

MUSICIANS

When the battleship fleet departed for the Pacific, the Navy Department, in order to secure long-term men for the trip, was obliged to call on the Navy Yard bands in order to obtain the full quota of musicians for the battleships. Nearly all of the bands at the several Eastern Navy Yards were more or less depleted, but it was thought there would be no serious difficulties in filling the places made vacant in the yard bands. This, however, did not prove correct, and according to Boston papers the band at that yard was left with but one musician who could play a brass instrument.

A few years ago bandsmen were enlisted for special service and allowed to go home each night, to go to and from the yard in civilian clothing and to work outside when not employed in the yard.

According to a Boston paper, the Navy Department has directed that bandsmen can be enlisted for the regular four-year term of enlistment, and that official contracts can be made with them that they will not be ordered to sea or from the station where they enlisted for two years. Other technical provisions and promises in the order mean that they can also avoid continuing in the service if ordered to sea after two years, either by one or two official courses.

CHANGES DURING APRIL

Ratings: W. J. Ragas, electrician, third class, to second class; A. J. Holten, electrician, second class, to first class; T. F. Calhoun, master-at-arms, third class, to second class; F. T. Walling, gunner's mate, third class, to second class; W. X. Garren, carpenter's mate, second class, to first class; S. Allary, carpenter's mate, third class, to second class; T. E. Chaffee, carpenter's mate, second class, to first class; E. Williams, ship's cook, third class, to mess attendant, second class; J. Lynch, watertender, to fireman, first class; C. J. S. Williams, ship's cook, fourth class, to third class; R. A. Young, electrician, first class, to chief electrician; O. C. Sanford, seaman, to coxswain.

Received from U. S. S. West Virginia: Ah Sing, wardroom cook.

Transferred: W. Denny, boilermaker; N. J. Wolf, baker, second class; H. Wormley, wardroom cook; D. A. Grabill, oiler, and G. H. Hanson, ordinary seaman, to Hospital at Navy Yard, Puget Sound, Wash.; R. J. Fitch, seaman, to U. S. S. West Virginia; B. F. Jackson, private, to Marine Barracks, Navy Yard, Puget Sound.

The Brand-New Rook to His Hammock.

This is pretty close space for a man.
  Am I glad that I shipped? Well, I ain't.
I will make no complaint, for, by gosh!
  There is not even room for complaint.

CRUISING THROUGH WASHINGTON.

(Continued from Page 6)

largest salmon cannery in the world, labeled "Bellingham, Washington—Dear Dad: Here's where they make 'em." These were sent off to the vessels and distributed to the bluejackets.

The schools were closed in order to give the children of the city a chance to see Uncle Sam's fighting machines, and the ships were crowded with visitors during the entire stay.

It was with regret that the Second Division left Bellingham.

On April 11th, at 8 a. m., the ships proceeded to Blaine, Washington, arriving there at 11 a. m., a distance of about thirty-seven miles. Blaine is a small city, located almost on the border line between Canada and the United States. The town has a population of about 2,800. A royal welcome was given to the officers and men, and a general holiday was declared in order that all of the school children and citizens might visit the men-of-war, which they did with eagerness until the ships left for Everett, a short stay at Blaine being necessary on account of other places on the itinerary.

Previous to leaving Blaine a telegram was received by the Division Commander from the Mayor of Anacortes, requesting that if possible the vessels pass through Guemes Channel. The Division Commander very kindly complied with the request and the citizens of Anacortes were thus enabled to obtain a passing view of two of the best warships in the world.

A visit of one day was paid to the hustling little town of Everett, Washington, the ships arriving there at 4 p. m. on the 12th.

Everett, a thriving little town of 25,000 population, is the county seat of Snohomish County, and is located on the Northern Pacific, the Great Northern, and Monte Cristo railroads, about fifty-five miles east by north of Tacoma and thirty miles north of Seattle. It has an excellent harbor and water communication with Puget Sound and Pacific ports. Everett can boast of a very unusual combination, having agricultural lands, forests and mines nearby. It is the port of entry to a large mining district, and within a short distance are located the Monte Cristo, Great Lake, Silver Creek, Troublesome, Sultan, Stillaguamish and the North Fork District mines, all of which send their ores to the great smelters in Everett and thereby contribute naturally to the substantial growth of the city.

Everett is a thoroughly modern city, contains railroad shops, flour and lumber mills, factories, excellent schools, electric cars, etc., and is called the City of Smokestacks from the large number of manufactories and smelters located there.

Everett was not founded until 1890, and when today one views the vast business enterprises and large section covered

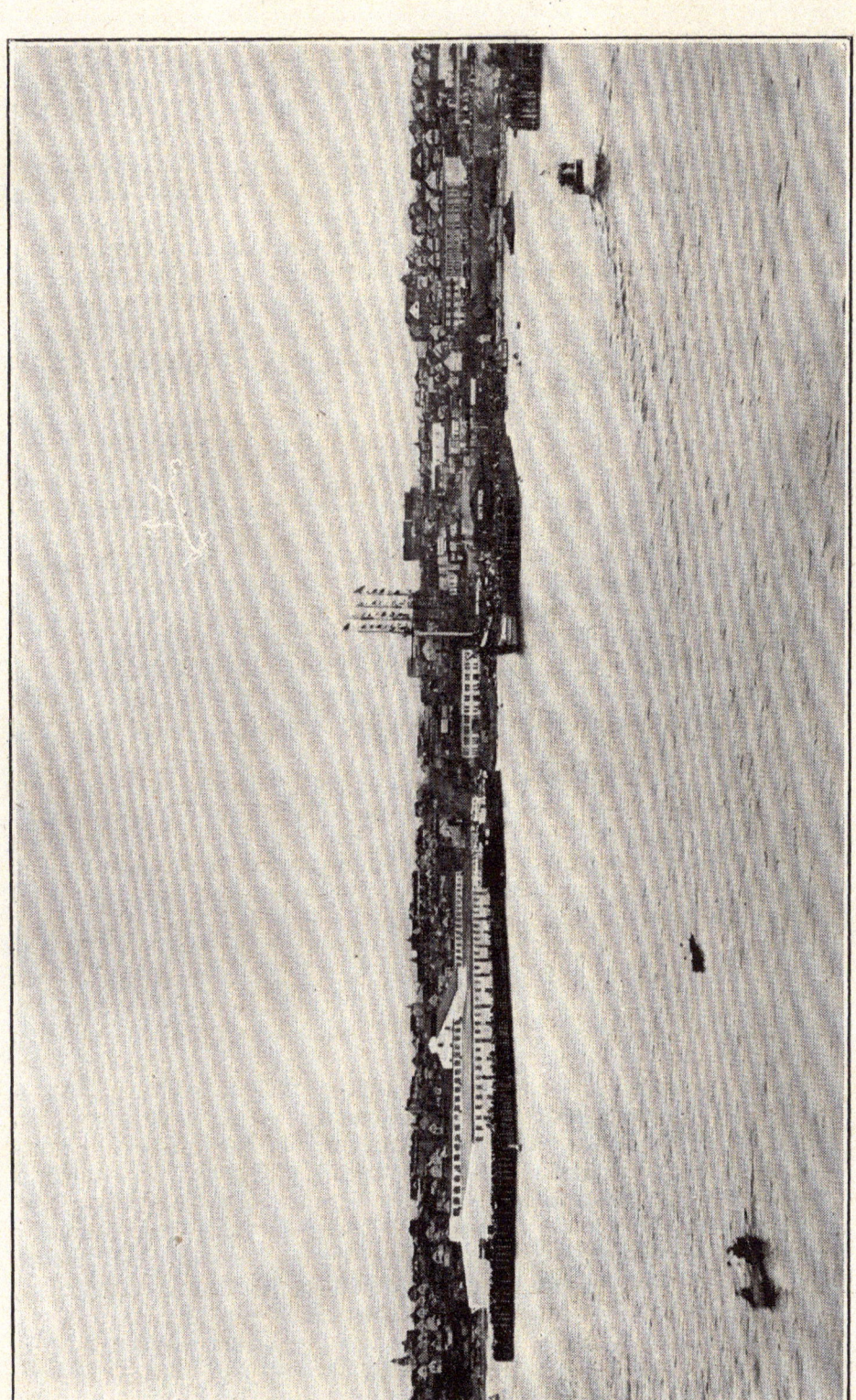

THRIVING CITY OF EVERETT, WASH. —*Photo by Varalla.*

by the growth of the city, it is almost inconceivable that less than 18 years ago the city had not been founded.

Leaving Everett at 2 p. m., the Tennessee and California steamed to Seattle, the metropolis of Washington, joining the U. S. S. Washington. Seattle is a large and beautiful city, in an ideal location, with an almost perfect drainage. This city is the port of entry of the State and is located on Puget Sound, 129 miles inland from the Pacific Ocean and 804 miles by water from San Francisco. It is the terminal point of the transcontinental railways, and it is here that steamers may be taken for Asiatic, Pacific, Canadian or Alaskan ports. The city fronts on Elliott Bay, which forms an extensive deep-water harbor four miles long and two miles wide, easily accessible and a shelter for the largest vessels in all kinds of weather. On the east side is Lake Washington, a fresh body of water twenty-two miles long, two to four miles wide and of great depth. Lake Union and Green Lake are also located within the city limits.

The city of Seattle is hilly, some of the elevations rising 300 feet above the sea level. The scenery surrounding this place is magnificent, including in one view the waters and green islands of Puget Sound, Lake Washington and the Olympic and Cascade Mountains. The snow-capped domes of Mount Tacoma (or Rainier) and Mount Baker extend along the eastern horizon, the intervening country being covered with green fields.

The climate is delightful, the temperature in summer never exceeding 90 degrees and in winter never as low as zero. The temperature has been as low as 12 above zero but once in three years, while the average temperature for December and January is about 40 degrees and for July and August 72 degrees.

The Alaska trade is extensive, there being twelve regular lines of steamships established, having twelve regular vessels weekly during the summer and six to eight weekly in winter. This is the home port of the Great Northern Steamship Company.

Seattle covers twenty-eight square miles. There are a number of public parks of great natural beauty and a system of boulevards running along the shores of the lakes and connecting all the parks into one system. Fort Lawton, with a large garrison, is within the city limits. Moran Brothers' Shipbuilding Company is located here, having but recently completed the large and magnificent battleship Nebraska. The city is well connected with Tacoma and surrounding towns by an excellent traction system.

What is now Seattle was formerly the home of many hundred Indians and was the meeting-place of many tribes. Pioneers first settled in 1852 under what is known as the "Donation Act of Congress, 1850." In 1853 the town was laid out and named "Seattle," after a friendly Indian chief.

The population in 1870 was 1,107, but with the entrance of the railroads in 1884 came the increase in population. On June 6, 1889, a terrific fire broke out, destroying the main portion of the city, burning 100 acres and causing damage to the extent of $10,000,000. In 1903 the population was estimated to be 121,813, in 1905 over 150,000, and today the Seattle Times claims 276,000. Thus it can be seen from this rapid growth the advantages possessed by Seattle as a commercial center.

In cities the size of Seattle the coming and going of men-of-war are very nearly everyday events, but a warm reception was given to the Second Division in spite of this. On April 13th the ships were illuminated from 8 to 9:30 p. m. and presented a very beautiful appearance when viewed from the hilltops of the city.

On April 14th the Washington got under way and proceeded to Tacoma, the Tennessee and California remaining at Seattle until April 15th, when the California proceeded to Bremerton for coal, the Tennessee remaining in Seattle until April 16th, when she left for Tacoma, joining the U. S. S. Washington at 2:30 o'clock that afternoon.

The reception accorded the ships at Tacoma was a grand one. Besides a ball for the entertainment of officers and men and an athletic contest, both of which are described on other pages, minor details for the entertainment and comfort of the men were carefully looked after, and it is safe to say that there was nothing further to be done in the line of entertainment for the enlisted men while in Tacoma.

The city of Tacoma has a population of about 100,000, although the census credits it with about 70,000; but, like other Washington cities, it is rapidly growing and in another decade bids fair to rival some of the large Eastern cities.

It is located on Commencement Bay and Puyallup River, twenty-eight miles south of Seattle and twenty-five miles north of Olympia, the capital, and is called the City of Destiny on account of its phenomenal growth. It is the head of navigation on Puget Sound and is a railroad center. The river empties into Commencement Bay within the city limits and forms a fine natural harbor. The Olympic Mountains stretch along to the west, while to the east is Mount Rainier, generally known as Mount Tacoma. The streets are level and very wisely laid out, so that there is not one less than eighty feet in width, and several beautiful avenues exceed one hundred feet in width. The residence section of the city is beautiful, nearly all of the homes being surrounded by fine lawns.

Tacoma was laid out in 1868 and has been known under the names of Old Town, Old Tacoma and New Tacoma until 1883, when it was given the name of Tacoma and has retained it since.

The first complete cargo ever taken from Tacoma was in 1869, but today there are twenty-five steamers which run regularly to the Orient alone, besides lines to Alaska and Pacific Coast ports.

There are two beautiful parks—the Wright, containing sixty acres, and Point Defiance Park, containing 662 acres.

This city is the seat of education for the State of Washington, having Washington College, Puget Sound University, Pacific University, Wright Seminary, Whitworth College, Vashon College, Tacoma Academy and the Academy of Visitation. There are seventy-one church buildings of various denominations.

On April 18th the Tennessee and Washington were illuminated in order that the citizens of Tacoma might enjoy the same sight as Seattle by viewing two of the finest ships in the world at night.

On April 19th, at 1 p. m., the Tennessee and Washington bade farewell to Tacoma and left for the Puget Sound Navy Yard, arriving there at a few minutes past 4 o'clock.

There were seventeen ships of various classes, both in and out of commission, prior to the arrival of the Tennessee and Washington, which will serve as a fair idea of the magnitude of this Navy Yard as a repair station. Many millions of dollars have been expended at this yard and it is one of the most thoroughly equipped repair stations in the country, employing at the present time about 2,100 men. There is a fine drydock, capable of accommodating any of the present-day ships, it being necessary for vessels repaired at Mare Island (of the largest type) to come to Puget Sound for docking in a Government dock. The dock is 637 feet long, 39 feet deep, 67 feet wide at the bottom and 130 feet at the top. The ships present are: Battleships—Wisconsin, Oregon, Nebraska; cruisers—Pennsylvania, Colorado, St. Louis, Milwaukee, Maryland, Tennessee, Washington, West Virginia, Boston; torpedo boats—Rowan, Goldsboro; gunboats—Wheeling and Princeton; collier—Saturn; receiving ship—Philadelphia; prison ship—Nipsic. Port Orchard and Charleston, with populations of 1,900, 750 and 600, respectively, are the places of residence of most of the mechanics employed at the Navy Yard.

The U. S. S. South Dakota reported for duty with the Second Division, U. S. Pacific Fleet, on April 15th, thereby completing the Second Division for the first time since its formation.

On April 23rd the Division Commander shifted his flag from the Tennessee to the California, and with the South Dakota proceeded to Anacortes, Wash., for a short visit, returning to the Navy Yard on April 27th, when he again transferred his flag to the Tennessee, the Second Division remaining at the Navy Yard until the end of the month.

THE SOCIAL WHIRL

On Thursday evening, April 9th, the citizens of Bellingham gave a delightful dance in Swanton's Dancing Academy at Lake Whatcom in honor of the officers and men of the Second Division. A few officers and fully 250 bluejackets from each vessel attended.

Although dancing commenced at 8:30 p. m., the full quota of bluejackets did not arrive until 10 o'clock, and after that time the reception committee was kept busy introducing the bluejackets to the Bellingham young ladies.

A large crowd of civilians attended and there was no lack of enthusiasm, as every dance was encored again and again. The galleries were packed with spectators who viewed the novel scene until after midnight, when the crowd broke up and the bluejackets returned to their respective ships, voting the citizens of Bellingham all jolly good fellows and the dance one of the finest attended for a good many days.

The Bellingham American of the 10th contained the following interesting item:

"The fair sex, young and old, turned out in force to the dance, and all the sailors who desired to dance found plenty of partners. The men in civilian dress had no chance to secure many dances against the array of sailor boys with their baggy blouses and big collars. The old saying of "Jack is at home wherever he goes" proved to be true, for he frequently visited the punch bowl with his partner and all of them mingled with the jolly crowd."

'Twas up in Bellingham we met;
   She gave me such a grand embrace;
Try as I will, I can't forget
   Her raven ringlets 'gainst my face.

We never had been introduced,
   And yet it lacked apparent harm;
She seemed to be indifferent
   As I grasped her quickly in my arms.

The maid had not mistaken me,
   I was a stranger in the town;
You see, 'twas in a skating rink
   We met as I was falling down.

GRAND BALL AT TACOMA

The Tacoma Fraternal Military Council gave a grand ball to the officers and enlisted men of the U. S. S. Tennessee and U. S. S. Washington at Tacoma on Friday evening, April 18th.

The ball was held in Dreamland Rink, corner of South and Eleventh Streets, and a crowd of 1,700 jolly Tacomans, officers and enlisted men were present to participate in the festivities.

The hall presented a very brilliant appearance, the gold lace and blue contrasting beautifully with the civilian dress of the Tacoma ladies and gentlemen.

At 9 o'clock the grand march was formed, and with over eight hundred in line, Admiral Sebree led off with Mrs. Sydney Plummer on his arm.

Through the kindness of the members of the Fraternal Military Council, who acted as floor committee, there was no lack of partners or enthusiasm, the numbers being encored again and again.

Captain Thomas B. Howard of the Tennessee and Captain Austin M. Knight of the Washington were present.

The following is an extract of the account in the Tacoma Ledger of April 19th:

"There was not a hitch in the plans. Five hundred or more sailors from the two cruisers were on shore leave and at Dreamland. Every member of the Tacoma Fraternal Military Council acted on the floor committee, and apparently not one sailor lacked a partner. It is estimated by the committee in charge that at least 1,700 persons were present. Captain Knight of the Washington and Captain Howard of the Tennessee smiled their approval of the happy throng from the gallery.

"The democratic air which prevailed caused no end of comment. Traditions that naval officers will not mingle with their men, just as plain American citizens, when not on duty, were upset.

"Music was furnished by the First Regiment Band, Uniform Rank, Knights of Pythias, under direction of Professor Kelley, and nineteen numbers, with three extras thrown in, were hardly finished before it was time for officers and men to return to their ships."

The dedication of the dance numbers is shown by the following program:

Grand March.."To Our Admiral"
Waltz.."To the Men Behind the Guns"
Two-Step.."To the Boys on the Ships"
Three-Step ...."To Our President, Teddy Roosevelt"
Quadrille, Lanciers ...."To the Governor, Albert E. Mead"
Dewey Two-Step ...."You May Fire When Ready"

TENNESSEE'S MINSTRELS. —*Photo by Varalla.*

Waltz ...."To the Navy"
French Minuet ...."To the Army"
Waltz ...."To All Fraternal Military Organizations"
Three-Step ...."To Our Insular Possessions"

INTERMISSION.

Two-Step ...."There Will be a Hotter Time if More Trouble Comes"
Schottische..............................."To the City of Destiny"
Germania Waltz.................................."To the Officers"
Two-Step ...."To the Chamber of Commerce"
Waltz, Ladies' Choice...................."To the Battle of Manila Bay"
Three-Step ...."To the Battle of Santiago"
Two-Step ...."Shore Leave"
Waltz ...."Home, Sweet Home"
Extra ...."You are Welcome, Come Again"
Extra ...."To Mayor Wright"
Extra ...."To Judge Linck, Our Next Mayor"

On April 24th the Washington gave a beautiful ball to the citizens of Seattle. A number of officers and men from each vessel were invited and the affair was thoroughly enjoyed by all.

TENNESSEE CARRIES OFF ATHLETIC HONORS

On Saturday evening, April 19th, before the Y. M. C. A. of Tacoma, the crews of the Tennessee and Washington engaged in one of the largest and most enthusiastic indoor athletic meets ever held in Tacoma. The event took place in the Glide Rink and resulted in a walkover for the Tennessee by a score of 61 to 17. The Washington team, though a game loser and sorely disappointed in not being able to carry off the honors in the State for which their ship was named, cheered lustily the winner of each event, showing their true sportsmanship.

The Tennessee team went ashore to win, headed by the Tennessee's Brass Band. The entries were well filled and the team as a whole performed remarkably well, having received notice of the meet only twenty-four hours previously.

The crowd numbered over 1,000, and a great many men from each vessel went ashore to cheer their shipmates on to victory. The Washington chose the south side of the hall to station the men who were to prove that their lung capacity was not wanting, and the Tennessee chose the north side, each crew having a large banner bearing the name of the ship.

ATHLETIC TROPHIES WON BY U. S. S. TENNESSEE, AT TACOMA, WASH. —*Photo by Varalla.*

De Witt M. Evans acted as umpire.
The following is a summary of the events:

	Points.	
	Tennessee.	Washington.
Indoor Baseball Game—		
Tennessee 18, Washington 2..............	5	
Thirty-five Yard Dash—		
Lieut. J. D. WILLSON....Tennessee, first	5	
SNYDER ....Washington, second		3
BLAHOS .. ..Tennessee, third	1	
High Jump—		
DAVIDSON ....Tennessee, first	5	
JONES ....Tennessee, second	3	
GARRON ....Tennessee, third	1	
Putting the Shot—		
G. AUSTIN ....Tennessee, first	5	
LAFFERTY ....Washington, second		3
SMITH ....Tennessee, third	1	
Three-legged Race—		
COSTELLO and WEINSTEIN.........first	5	
REY and HOUGHTON............second	3	
STEIN and CRAMER..............third	1	
All of Tennessee.		
Wheelbarrow Race—		
BURKHART and FARRALL..Wash., first		5
BIRX and JONES......Tennessee, second	3	
WELSON and DELAN........Wash., third		1
Tug of War—		
TENNESSEE (Austin, anchor).... first	5	
Sack Race—		
MAYS ....Tennessee, first	5	
REEKS ....Tennessee, second	3	
O'GRADY ....Tennessee, third	1	
Potato Race—		
LAFFERTY ....Washington, first		5
DALY .. ..Tennessee, second	3	
KENNITZER .. ..Tennessee, third	1	
Relay Race—		
TENNESSEE ....first	5	
Total points..........	61	17

The winner of each event was presented with a medal, and the Tennessee was also presented with a beautiful silver loving-cup by the Tacoma Chamber of Commerce.

The Tennessee team performed in an excellent manner, having received notice of the event only a short time previous to the time set, and the excellent spirit of the crew was shown to a good advantage in bringing back the prizes.

THE VOLUNTEER

DAILY LOG FOR APRIL

Wednesday, 1st—Sailed from San Francisco for Port Angeles, Wash.

Thursday, 2nd—At sea, en route to Port Angeles, Wash.

Friday, 3rd—At sea, en route to Port Angeles, Wash.

Saturday, 4th—At sea until 4:21 a. m., when anchored in Port Angeles. Official calls exchanged with Commanding Officers and city officials. Visitors on board. Liberty party ashore.

Sunday, 5th—At Port Angeles. Visitors on board. Liberty party ashore. Usual Sunday quarters and inspection.

Monday, 6th—At Port Angeles until 10 a. m.; proceeded to Port Townsend and anchored at 1:45 p. m. Chamber of Commerce and Colonel Cummings, Commandant Fort Worden, called. Visitors on board. Liberty party ashore.

Tuesday, 7th—At Port Townsend. Official calls exchanged with British Vice-Consul. Division Commander and Commanding Officers called on Chamber of Commerce and Colonel Cummings, Commandant Fort Worden. Visitors on board. Liberty party ashore. Reception and dance given on shore in honor of ships.

Wednesday, 8th—At Port Townsend until 9 a. m.; got under way and anchored in Bellingham, Wash., at 1:30 p. m. Washington went to Seattle. Chamber of Commerce called. Liberty party ashore.

Thursday, 9th—At Bellingham. Ship thronged with visitors. Party ashore to attend ball given in honor of ships.

Friday, 10th—At Bellingham. Visitors aboard. Liberty party ashore.

Saturday, 11th—At Bellingham until 7:56 a. m.; proceeded to Blaine, Wash.; anchored at 11:02 a. m. Visitors on board. Holiday in Blaine in honor of ships. Liberty party ashore.

Sunday, 12th—At Blaine until 7:54 a. m.; got under way, passed through Guemes Channel in order to give citizens of Anacortes a chance to see ships, and anchored in Everett, Wash., at 3:50 p. m. Exchanged calls with Chamber of Commerce. Ship thronged with visitors. Liberty party ashore.

Monday, 13th—At Everett until 2 p. m.; proceeded to Seattle and anchored at 4:50 p. m. Usual Sunday quarters and inspection. Visitors aboard. Liberty party ashore. Ship illuminated during the evening. Reception on Washington, attended by officers; Governor of State present.

Tuesday, 14th—At Seattle. Visitors aboard. Liberty party ashore. Washington left for Tacoma.

Wednesday, 15th—At Seattle. Liberty party ashore. California left for Bremerton to coal. Visitors aboard. South Dakota joined Second Division.

Thursday, 16th—At Seattle. Liberty party ashore.

Friday, 17th—At Seattle until 1 p. m.; proceeded to Tacoma and anchored at 3:24 p. m. Official calls exchanged with Commanding Officer of Washington and Chamber of Commerce. Sent party ashore to attend ball given by citizens of Tacoma in honor of ships.

Saturday, 18th—At Tacoma. Large number of visitors on board. Ship illuminated during evening. Sent athletic party ashore; won cup presented by Tacoma Chamber of Commerce.

Sunday, 19th—At Tacoma until 1 p. m., when, with Washington, left for Puget Sound Navy Yard, anchoring at 3:40 p. m. Division Commander called on Commandant. Maryland arrived at 5:30 p. m.

Monday, 20th—At Navy Yard. Official calls exchanged between ships present and Commandant. Rigged coaling gear. Saluted Commandant, thirteen guns.

Tuesday, 21st—At Navy Yard. Coaling ship. Took on 1,900 tons.

Wednesday, 22nd—Cleaning up. Liberty party ashore. At 5 p. m. Division Commander shifted flag to California.

Thursday, 23rd—At Navy Yard. California and South Dakota left for Anacortes. West Virginia arrived.

Friday, 24th—At Navy Yard. Sent liberty party ashore. Grand ball and minstrel show given in Seattle by U. S. S. Washington.

Saturday, 25th—At Navy Yard. Field day. Sent liberty party ashore.

Sunday, 26th—At Navy Yard. Usual quarters and inspection. Sent liberty party ashore.

Monday, 27th—At Navy Yard. Landed battalion. Boxing contests on board in evening. Boxing: Frommer vs. Hoskins; Simons vs. Carr. Wrestling match: White vs. Jones; White won. No decisions rendered in boxing. Officers from ships and yard and fifteen men from each ship invited.

Tuesday, 28th—At Navy Yard. Landing party ashore for drill. Sent liberty party ashore. Rear Admiral Clark called.

Wednesday, 29th—At Navy Yard. Landing party ashore. Preparing for sea.

Thusday, 30th—At Navy Yard. Liberty party ashore. Preparing for sea.

Smoking to some people may be injurious, but it improves hams.

SOME OF THE BOYS WHO KEEP THE TENNESSEE NEATEST OF ALL. —*Photo by Varalla.*

IN THE SWIM

Of all the pleasures that I know,
This does my soul elate,
To hear reveille at half-past five
And then sleep in till eight.

At the Bellingham Dance.

A certain boatswain's mate: "My! the floor is slippery. It is hard to keep on your feet."

She: "Then you are trying to keep on my feet? I thought it was accidental."

In the Skating Rink at Seattle.

A certain C. P. O., as he flops: "Beg pardon, but aren't we acquainted?"

She: "At any rate, it is not a long-standing acquaintance."

Alcohol may be food, but why eat between meals?

One of the best remedies for a good appetite is food.

John Livermore on the Washington is fourth class. He will now Liver-more correct life.

It is far better to make a collection of steins, as C. P. is doing, than to make a collection of what comes in them.

The land-lubber author in a late sea story: "The sailor swept the horizon"—but he did not use the Tennessee's brooms.

"Stick it out," boys! The Mayor of Timpson, Texas, receives a salary of $1 per annum, and there is talk of reducing it to 60 cents.

Oh to be shipmates with that ex-bluejacket who wrote a certain service paper that one of the greatest pleasures of a man-of-warsman was "scrubbing his clothes."

"There isn't much to eat," said the Port Angeles restaurant keeper on Sunday morning as he absent-mindedly set out a candle—"only light refreshments."

Some of the overtimers waiting for the morning boat: "Day is breaking."

Witty Willie from the Second Division: "Well, we beat day; we have been broke two hours."

ITINERARY—U. S. S. TENNESSEE

Port	Arrival	Departure	Miles
League Island, Pa. (con's'd)	July 17, '06	Nov. 1, '06	233
Hampton Roads, Va.	Nov. 3, "	" 8, "	98
Piney Point, Md.	" 8, "	" 8, "	1834
Colon, Panama	" 14, "	" 15, "	130
Chiriqui Lagoon	" 16, "	" 16, "	1041
Ponce, Porto Rico	" 21, "	" 22, "	1285
Hampton Roads, Va.	" 26, "	Dec. 16, "	240
League Island, Pa.	Dec. 18, "	Apr. 12, '07	233
Hampton Roads, Va.	Apr. 13, '07	" 14, "	15
Lynn Haven Bay, Va.	" 14, "	" 16, "	16
Hampton Roads, Va.	" 16, "	May 16, "	530
Provincetown, Mass.	May 18, "	" 24, "	53
Boston, Mass.	" 25, "	June 5, "	555
Hampton Roads, Va.	June 7, "	" 11, "	382
Newport, R. I.	" 12, "	" 14, "	3112
Royan, France	" 23, "	July 2, "	52
Ile D' Aix, France	July 2, "	" 3, "	10
La Rochelle, France	" 3, "	" 11, "	235
Brest, France	" 12, "	" 25, "	3194
Tompkinsville, S. I.	Aug. 6, "	Aug. 16, "	270
Hampton Roads, Va.	" 17, "	" 17, "	392
Newport, R. I.	" 18, "	" 19, "	265
Boston, Mass.	" 20, "	Sept. 30, "	265
Newport, R. I.	Oct. 1, "	Oct. 4, "	392
Hampton Roads, Va.	" 5, "	" 12, "	1904
Port of Spain, Trinidad	" 18, "	" 24, "	3300
Rio de Janeiro, Brazil	Nov. 4, "	Nov. 10, "	1044
Montevideo, Uruguay	" 13, "	" 19, "	1325
Punta Arenas, Chile	" 23, "	" 27, "	2760
Callao, Peru	Dec. 5, "	Dec. 12, "	2240
Acapulco, Mexico	" 19, "	" 22, "	785
Pichilinque Bay, Mexico	" 25, "	" 28, "	315
Magdalena Bay, Mexico	" 29, "	Feb. 15, '08	1026
San Francisco, Cal.	Feb. 20, '08	" 29, "	287
Santa Barbara, Cal.	Mar. 1, "	Mar. 6, "	164
San Diego, Cal.	" 6, "	" 16, "	96
San Pedro, Cal.		" 23, "	18
Redondo, Cal.			9

The Saturday Evening Post

A CLEAN, THOROUGHLY UP-TO-DATE WEEKLY BRIMFUL of BRIGHT NEWS and GOOD STORIES

Cosmopolitan
Motor
Metropolitan
Pearson's
Ainslee's
Argosy
Broadway
Burr McIntosh
Collier's Weekly
Everybody's
Judge
Leslie's Weekly
Life
Outing
Review of Reviews
Scientific American
Scrap Book
Smart Set
Success
Sunset
Travel Magazine
World's Work
Our Navy
Red Book
Blue Book
Popular

Clowry
QUARTERMASTER

WHAT YOU DO NOT SEE — ASK FOR

Has them all

Novelty Knives and Razors Any name, ship, photo or emblem you desire on handles. Prices from 80 cents up. Goods guaranteed

ALBERT E. AUGER, Engineer's Storeroom

The Volunteer

BOOK SIX

The Volunteer

JULY, 1908

Published Monthly Aboard the U. S. S. Tennessee

Obituary

Wood, George. Water Tender. Born, Yorkshire, England. Age, 41 years 5 months. Enlisted, Philadelphia, April 20, 1906. Previous naval service, 10 years.

Boggs, Earle Claton. Fireman, second class. Born, Arondale, Alabama. Age, 18 years. Enlisted Birmingham, Alabama, April 27, 1907.

Meek, George Waddle. Fireman, second class. Born, Scotland. Age, 27 years 3 months. Enlisted St. Louis, Mo., October 6, 1906.

Reinhold, Adolph. Machinist's mate, second class. Born, Germany. Age, 28 years 2 months. Enlisted at Saginaw, Mich., August 28, 1907.

Burns, Edward Joseph. Coal passer. Born, Brooklyn, N. Y. Age, 25 years 6 months. Enlisted New York, N. Y., August 7, 1907.

Carroll, John Patrick Anthony. Fireman, second class. Born, Hartford, Conn. Age, 23 years. Enlisted at Hartford, Conn., May 22, 1906.

Maxfield, Fredric Sardin. Fireman, second class. Born, Toughkena, Penn. Age, 22 years 10 months. Enlisted at New York, N. Y., September 16, 1906.

U. S. S. Tennessee in Dry-Dock at Hunter's Point,
San Francisco, Cal.

THE VOLUNTEER
for July, 1908

OUR CRUISE

THE Tennessee and California, having spent the interval between Friday and Monday at Venice, Cal., got underway at 10.30 a. m. and sailed for Point Dume, where the remaining vessels of the Second Division and the First Division had rendezvoused, and all of the ships, except the Pennsylvania flying the flag of the Commander-in-Chief, which left the formation to continue Admiral's inspection, steamed into Santa Barbara harbor and anchored about six o'clock. Shortly afterward the Pennsylvania came in and anchored, the Commander-in-Chief transferring his flag to the West Virginia.

A party of inspecting officers reported on board to assist the Division Commander in the inspection of the Tennessee and on the 3rd inspection was begun. The Admiral's inspection in these progressive days means more than the inspection of a few years ago, since every portion of the ship from stem to stern is thoroughly examined, all equipment and supplies are looked over and all drills and evolutions must be performed both at anchor and underway.

As the Tennessee is ready for inspection at almost any time it was only necessary to attend to a few minor details, which were completed early in the day. The Division Commander and inspecting officers started at 9 a. m., the crew being at quarters. The inspection continued during the 3rd, 4th and part of the 5th.

The vessels of the First Squadron were assigned to the following ports to give liberty from the 5th to the 8th: Washington to Venice; West Virginia, Colorado and California to Redondo; Tennessee to San Pedro; Maryland and Pennsylvania to Long Beach.

The Tennessee got underway on Friday, the 5th, at 9 a. m. ahead of the remaining vessels of the Squadron, in order to complete Admiral's inspection on the run to San Pedro, and proceeded outside of Santa Barbara. The full power speed trial required by navy regulations was in progress and the splendid fighting machine was behaving admirably. The turns made indicated a speed of 21 knots and was climbing. As the revolutions increased smiles of contentment spread over the countenances of the many men who are proud of the excellent qualifications of the great ship. Finally top speed was reached and pressure was being reduced, when all of a sudden a 4-inch boiler tube in boiler G, fire-room No. 3, burst and with full force the bulk of steam rushed out into the compartment, catching some of the firemen, others barely managing to escape.

Fire quarters sounded and all hands went promptly to their stations. As soon as entrance could be gained to the fire-room it was found that the following men had been killed almost instantly: G. Wood, water-tender; E. C. Boggs, coal passer; Adolph Reinhold, machinist's mate, second class; and G. W. Meek, fireman, first class; the following were terribly injured: F. S. Maxfield, fireman, second class; S. Stamatis, fireman, 1st class; E. J. Burns, coal passer; W. S. Burns, coal passer; J. P. A. Carroll, fireman, second class; H. Fitzpatrick, fireman, first class; G. M. Corns, fireman, second class; A. Hayes, water-tender; R. F. Rutledge, coal passer; R. W. Watson, fireman, second class.

The Division Commander and Senior Engineer Officer had just finished an inspection of some of the after fire-rooms and were about to ascend, passing through the port engine room, when a man rushed madly past for the ladder. It was apparent that an accident had happened and the boilers in the locality were quickly cut out and furnace fire extinguishers turned on, steam falling almost immediately. The crew was cool and collected, some of the men displaying remarkable courage in entering the fire-room in the midst of the escaping steam and water, rescuing the injured and tenderly removing them to the sick bay, where everything possible was done to relieve the terrible suffering.

Communication was established with the First Division, which steamed full speed to the rescue and sent medical aid and supplies. As soon as possible, the Tennessee steamed full speed toward San Pedro, in the meantime communicating by wireless with Los Angeles and making arrangements for the transfer of the injured by special car to a hospital. Upon arrival at San Pedro, it was decided not to send the men to the hospital until the following morning.

The horrible accident was not without its effect upon the crew. What was a happy and care free ship's company a few moments before was now sad and grief stricken men with bowed heads, deep in thought for the welfare of shipmates.

Upon an examination of the tube, a small hole, less than seven inches in length, was found, and one would indeed have to stretch the imagination to think that a few moments before this same harmless looking place had extinguished the flame of life in four able-bodied men, and probably fatally injured eight or ten more, yet such was the case.

This was the first serious accident to mar the excellent record of the Tennessee. During the long run from Hampton Roads and through preliminary and record target practice at Magdalena Bay not a man was even severely injured, and the blow came like a crash, almost too sudden to be realized until one had time to think over the terrible situation.

At 6.10 a. m. on the 6th, after suffering untold pain, E. J. Burns, coal passer, died. The remaining men, with the exception of Corns, Rutledge and Watson, were transferred to shore, thence in special car to a hospital at Los Angeles, where everything possible was done to maintain life. J. P. A. Carroll died at 10.20 p. m. that night, and F. S. Maxfield died at 10.20 a. m. the following morning.

On June 6th, at 1.30 p. m., funeral services were held over the remains of the men who had died on board from the terrible accident of the day before. Sad indeed was the ceremony over the remains of our beloved shipmates, and as each was lowered into a waiting cutter, while the band played a dirge, one was forced to realize that life at its best is but a thread, and those who are well and strong today are not sure of tomorrow. Colors were half-masted during the services and the funeral procession steamed to San Pedro dock, where the bodies were removed to the shore and the procession proceeded to the little cemetery overlooking San Pedro harbor, where interment took place. Here, in the soil of the grand state of California, on a site overlooking the sea they loved so well, was the last resting place of the brave men who gave their lives for the country.

Services were again conducted on the 8th and 10th for F. S. Maxfield and J. P. A. Carroll, respectively, and they were laid side by side in the little cemetery with their brave shipmates. A large funeral party was present, besides many citizens.

The 6th of June was turned into a day of mourning by the good people of San Pedro, all stores and places of business were closed during the services and it is estimated that 3,000 people followed the funeral procession to the cemetery. The generous spirit and many offers of assistance by the kind people of San Pedro is indeed highly commendable and a worthy example for many other cities to follow. On June 13th, after a sad and grief stricken week spent at San Pedro, the Tennessee left, at 10 p. m., and proceeded to Santa Barbara, anchoring the following morning. Upon arrival, the West Virginia and Maryland departed for the Mare Island Navy Yard to undergo repairs, and at 3.55 that afternoon the Tennessee, leading the Second Division, steamed out of Santa Barbara and after an uneventful trip, anchored in Santa Cruz at 7.21 a. m. next day.

Santa Cruz, a city of about 5,700 population, is located on Monterey Bay, 30 miles from the city of that name and 62 miles from San Francisco. It is a delightful summer resort and contains all of the features of a modern amusement place, especially in a fine dance hall and skating rink, where the boys held forth in glee during the enjoyable liberty.

Many of the men took advantage of the beautiful trip to the large trees located in Redwood, about 8 miles from Santa Cruz. An impressive example of the modern bluejacket was discernable in the number of automobile and driving parties enjoying the beauties of nature on one of the most picturesque pleasure trips that California has to offer.

Owing to the limited amount of time available, the Second Division got underway on the 13th, and after a very pleasant trip up the coast, through the Golden Gate and San Pablo Bay, anchored in Carquines Straits, off Mare Island Light, at 2.50 p. m. The West Virginia and Maryland had just left the anchorage and were going to Mare Island Navy Yard for repairs.

Mare Island, located about 29 miles from San Francisco, has one of the largest and finest navy yards of which the United States can boast. Anchored off the yard is the old-time Independence, which has a long and brilliant naval career, now serving as a receiving ship.

Information was received that the Tennessee would be put in dry-dock at Hunter's Point on the 20th, so on the 19th, we proceeded to San Francisco and anchored off the Union Iron Works, and on the 20th, at 5.32 p. m., entered the dry-dock at Hunter's Point.

The ship had not been docked since September, 1907, and as was expected, the bottom was rather foul, after the long cruise from the East coast and a lengthy stay in tropical waters. This was soon remedied by the hard working crew and after giving the underbody two coats of marine paint, the ship presented as fine an appearance as any of Uncle Sam's fighting machines; and on the 22nd, at 6.30 p. m., she again entered her native element, anchoring in San Francisco harbor.

The Tennessee remained in San Francisco harbor until June 30th, preparing for a practice cruise to Southward.

THE VOLUNTEER

PUBLISHED MONTHLY ABOARD THE U. S. S. TENNESSEE

J. E. ERWIN . . . . PUBLISHER

VOL. 1.   NO. 6   JULY, 1908   PRICE, 15 CENTS

OUR CAPTAIN

Captain Thomas B. Howard, U. S. Navy, who has been in command of the U. S. S. Tennessee since October 6, 1907, was detached on the 23rd instant and ordered to command the U. S. S. Ohio in the Atlantic Fleet.

We regret the loss of our able commanding officer and he goes to the battleship fleet with the best wishes of the entire crew of the U. S. S. Tennessee for his welfare and success.

★ ★ ★

CHANGES FOR JUNE, 1908

RATINGS.—W. H. Gowan, coxswain to boatswain's mate, second class; A. Wrightson, quartermaster, third class, to second class; W. E. Bond, ordinary seaman to seaman; D. C. McIlvaney, ordinary seaman to seaman; W. H. Evans, seaman to yeoman, third class; R. Mergans, seaman to coxswain; F. S. Myers, ordinary seaman to seaman; H. G. Heitkotter, shipwright to carpenter's mate, third class; L. M. Bales, carpenter's mate, third class, to second class.

TRANSFERS.—S. Stamatis, fireman, first class; W. S. Burns, coal passer; A. Hayes, water tender; H. Fitzpatrick, fireman, first class; F. S. Maxfield, fireman, second class; J. P. A. Carroll, fireman, second class, to Marine Hospital, San Pedro, June 6th. G. M. Corns, fireman, second class; R. F. Rutledge, coal passer; A. J. Reams, ordinary seaman; F. Kuhn, ordinary seaman; J. C. Williams, coal passer; W. Gill, steerage cook; O. J. Matthieson, ordinary seaman, to Naval Hospital, Mare Island, June 24.

Additional Transfers.—W. C. Humphrey, ordinary seaman, to New Jersey, June 28. J. Brady, chief yeoman, to Justin for Alabama, June 4.

ENLISTMENTS.—June 10: H. E. Orcott, coal passer; J. Carr, musician, second class, at San Pedro.

DISCHARGES.—June 6: P. Gribbon, water tender; J. Cooley, coal passer; June 9: G. M. Gately, coal passer; June 22: C. D. Levandowski, musician, second class; June 27: J. E. Carter, electrician, third class.

RECEIVED —June 3, T. P. Byram, yeoman, third class, from Independence; June 18, Q. R. Thompson, quartermaster, second class, from Independence; June 19, A. N. Williams, yeoman, first class, from Pensacola; June 27, H. H. Melchert, ordinary seaman, from New Jersey; June 28, D. J. Kennedy, W. D. Adams, S. Billick, J. Lyon, E. S. Fetters, A. R. Garant, C. Hall, B. M. Haslett, privates, from Marine Barracks, Navy Yard, Mare Island, Cal.

★ ★ ★

MESS SEVENTY-ONE

Mess 71 just knows the way the Navy should be run—
They tell their shipmates day by day just what now should be done
They know how to give liberty, they have a simple plan
But when there is some work to do, it's "get some other man."

Blahos in a day or two could land big crooks in jail
There's nothing that he couldn't do, he knows no word like fail;
Our confidence he can maintain, of that there is no doubt,
But when the field days come around he's simply down and out.

All public questions Phillips grabs and settles on the spot
He waits not till the new wears off, but grabs them while they're hot;
In matters of ship discipline, he knows just what to do,
But the hardest job that he can find, is turn out by "turn to."

Harrington gets tired out at what law makers say
Why he is just the man they need, he never goes astray.
He went up to Los Angeles and tried to kid for fun—
If you want to know how he made out, why just ask Harrington.

In conversation that prize mess can do some wondrous things
They're built upon much wiser plans than Presidents or kings,
They always know the ins and outs of every deep transaction,
We look to them for theories, but somewhere else for action.

IN MEMORY OF OUR SHIPMATES

THE sunbeams gently kissed the hills on Santa Barbara Bay
    One bright and sunny morning in the merry month of June,
The armored cruiser Tennessee at anchor gently lay;
The band was playing bright and catchy tunes.
As "turn to" went, the happy lads went bravely to their tasks
With a feeling that, secure and safe from harm,
They labored for the noble cause of honored Uncle Sam,
The strength and fiower of the nation's arms.
It was Admiral's inspection in the grand Pacific Fleet,
The Tennessee appeared to be the pride
Of the eight huge ships assembled, finest cruisers of the deep,
A credit to the nation far and wide.
To comply with regulations we were going to make a run,
"A forced draft trial" at our very best;
So, at 10 a. m., the anchor up, the great propellors churned,
And we stood out of the harbor for the test.
We held "clear ship" and routine drills, then settled down to work,
We hoped to make the record of the fleet,
Each man went bravely to his post, already for the run,
Not expecting any accident to meet.
The steam gauge rose, the great ship shook and threw the spray about,
As she plunged on madly through the briny foam,
And soon the speed passed twenty knots, then almost twenty-two,
As the hands upon the indicator shown.
All of a sudden came a cry, the engines seemed to stop,
Then some poor scalded victims made a dash
To get out of that gleaming hell, an awful, awful death,
But soon all human aid for them was past.
A four-inch water tube of steel had burst in boiler G
Out the roaring steam and flame came like a shot,
The poor men bravely at their posts were caught full force by this,
And some of them were stricken on the spot.

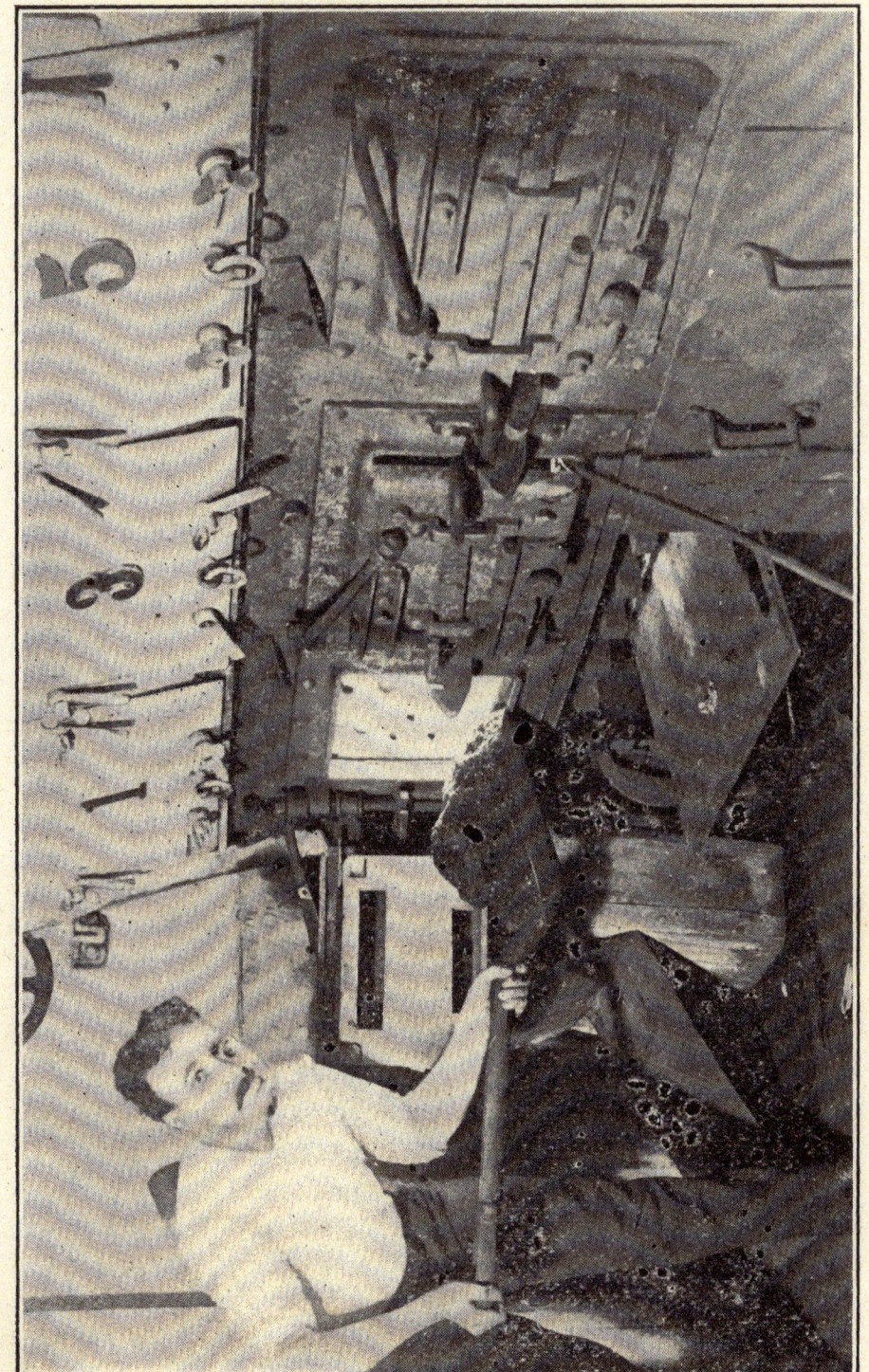

Fireroom No. 3, where the Accident Occurred

THE VOLUNTEER

Ah! soon 'twas o'er, the force was spent, brave men rushed madly in,
To rescue the ill-fated who were there,
Then tenderly they bore them to the sick-bay of the ship
To place them in the surgeon's kindly care.
The spark of life had flown from four, alas it was too late,
No earthly power could keep them from the grave,
But God will look through kindly eyes on death in country's cause
A noble life each manly fellow gave.
Though everything was done to ease the awful, stinging pain
Caused by that burning hell that leaped like mad,
The suffering was terrible, as they alone can tell,
Each shipmate, with bowed head, could feel but sad.
Next morning God claimed one more soul, that lingered through the night,
The remaining six then tenderly were borne,
To a nearby hospital on shore, the best that could be had;
But next day sad news came, two more had gone.
We gathered on the quarter-deck to say our last farewell;
Had our own kin died no sadder could it seem;
For even here there's brother love, when banded one and all
Into one of our country's great machines.
We gently laid them side by side in California's soil,
A few days and the cruiser sailed away,
But the memory of each shipmate will oft linger on the spot,
And revert with horror to that awful day.
Perhaps 'tis fate, at such a time, that plays the awful hand,
Yet for our human minds it's not to say;
The inevitable has always been and no doubt always will
Even though we near perfection day by day.
When all on earth are mustered at the judgment seat of God,
The great Tribunal, judge of all mankind,
We trust a place reserved will be, for men who died like this,
The greatest tribute of the human mind.
The dove of peace flies over all, no clouds are in our skies,
A life is all that any has to give,
But be it time of peace or war, he who on duty dies,
We hope eternally with God will live.

Big Four at Full Speed to Send Medical Aid

DAILY LOG FOR JUNE, 1908

1st, Monday. Partly cloudy and pleasant. At anchor, Venice, Cal., enroute for and at anchor in Santa Barbara, Cal. Got underway at 10.30 a. m., with U. S. S. California, and left for Santa Barbara. At 11.30 sighted First Division, Pacific Fleet, and at 12.56 p. m. joined same. The Commander-in-Chief transferred his flag to the Pennsylvania to proceed with the inspection of that vessel and left formation. Steamed into Santa Barbara and anchored at 5.01 p. m. Found Colorado and Washington in port coaling. At 6.50 p. m. the Pennsylvania entered the harbor and anchored at 7.35; the Commander-in-Chief transferred his flag to the West Virginia.

2nd, Tuesday. Fair and cool, hazy last part. At anchor, Santa Barbara. Baseball party ashore. West Virginia coaling from Justin. Justin shoved off at 3.20 p. m.

3rd, Wednesday. Fair and pleasant. At anchor, Santa Barbara. The Commander, Second Division, and party of inspecting officers started Admiral's inspection at 9 a. m. Baseball party ashore. Exercises by Christian Endeavor Society of Santa Barbara held on board. Searchlight drill. South Dakota sailed San Clemente Island.

4th, Thursday. Partly cloudy and pleasant, cool. At anchor, Santa Barbara. Having Admiral's inspection. California coaling from Justin until 4.00 p. m., when Justin sailed for San Francisco. Transferred J. Brady, Chief Yeoman, to Justin for further transfer to U. S. S. Alabama. T. P. Byram, yeoman, third class, received from Independence.

5th, Friday. Partly cloudy and warm; overcast last part. At anchor, Santa Barbara, underway for and at anchor in San Pedro, Cal. Got underway at 8.59 a. m. Having Admiral's inspection. Having general quarters and drills. At 11.15 4-inch water tube in Boiler G burst. The following men were killed instantly or died before reaching the sick bay: G. Wood, water tender; E. C. Boggs, fireman, 2nd class; A. Reinhold, machinist's mate, 2nd class; G. W. Meek, fireman, 1st class; the following men were injured: F. S. Maxfield, fireman, 1st

U. S. S. West Virginia Sending Medical Aid

class; S. Stamatis, fireman, 1st class; E. J. Burns, coal passer; W. S. Burns, coal passer; H. Fitzpatrick, fireman, 1st class; G. M. Corns, fireman, 2nd class; A. Hayes, watertender; R. F. Rutledge, coal passer; R. W. Watson, fireman, 2nd class. At 12.50 p. m. First Division ships came up, lowered life boats and sent medical aid and supplies. At 1.30 got underway full speed for San Pedro and anchored there at 5.35 p. m. South Dakota came in and anchored at 6.17 p. m. Commanding Officer South Dakota called officially on board.

6th, Saturday. Overcast and cloudy, clearing at night. At anchor, San Pedro. E. J. Burns, coal passer, injured in accident on June 5th, died at 6.15 a. m. Sent following injured men to hospital at Los Angeles: S. Stamatis, F. S. Maxfield, W. S. Burns, H. Fitzpatrick, J. P. A. Carroll, A. Hayes. At 1.30 p. m. held funeral services and sent funeral escort ashore with remains of men killed in accident of 5th instant. P. Gribbon, fireman, 1st class, honorably discharged upon expiration of four year term of enlistment. J. P. A. Carroll, fireman, 2nd class, died in Los Angeles Hospital at 10.20 p. m. from injuries received on June 5th.

7th, Sunday. Overcast and cloudy to partly cloudy and pleasant. At anchor, San Pedro. At 10.20 a. m., F. S. Maxfield, fireman, 2nd class, died in Los Angeles Hospital from injuries received on June 5th. Had usual Sunday quarters and inspection. Liberty party ashore.

8th, Monday. Partly cloudy and unpleasant. At anchor, San Pedro. At 9.00 a. m. U. S. S. Maryland passed and saluted with 13 guns, returned with 7. At 9.30 a. m. U. S. S. Pennsylvania stopped off San Pedro Breakwater and saluted with 13 guns; returned with 7. L. Turner, private, U.S.M.C., transferred to Pennsylvania. Sent funeral party ashore to attend funeral of F. S. Maxfield, fireman, 2nd class. Commanding Officer of the U. S. S. South Dakota called officially. Whaleboat from South Dakota capsized while under sail. Crew rescued by steam barge. Engaged in painting. Liberty party ashore.

9th, Tuesday. Fair and pleasant. Partly cloudy to over-

Fourth Division Bluejacket Band

cast. At anchor, San Pedro. Boat drill. G. M. Gately, coal passer, discharged. Liberty party ashore. South Dakota sailed.

10th, Wednesday. Overcast and cloudy. At anchor, San Pedro. At 9.10 p. m. sent funeral party ashore to attend funeral of J. P. A. Carroll, fireman, 2nd class. Divers working on strainers and propellors. Liberty party ashore.

11th, Thursday. Overcast and cloudy to partly cloudy and pleasant. Liberty party ashore.

12th, Friday. Partly cloudy and hazy. At anchor, San Pedro, enroute for Santa Barbara, Cal. At 7.30 a. m. Pacific Mail Steamer Curocoa entered harbor. Baseball party ashore. Lieutenant M. J. McCormack, U. S. N., reported for duty as Ordnance Officer by orders from Navy Department. Got underway at 10 p. m. and sailed for Santa Barbara, Cal.

13th, Saturday. Enroute for and at anchor in Santa Barbara, and enroute for Santa Cruz, Cal. Overcast and cloudy; cool. Passed four steamers. Entered Santa Barbara harbor and anchored at 5 29 a. m. Found following vessels in port: West Virginia, Maryland, Washington, California and South Dakota. At 10 a. m. West Virginia and Maryland sailed for San Francisco. The Commanding Officers, Washington, California and South Dakota called officially. At 3.55 p. m. the Second Division got underway and with Tennessee leading, in column, 500 yards distance, sailed for Santa Cruz, Cal.

14th, Sunday. Overcast and hazy to partly cloudy and cool. Enroute for and at anchor in Santa Cruz, Cal. At 6.10 adjusted compasses and steamed into Santa Cruz harbor, anchoring in identical column at 7.21 a. m. Had usual Sunday quarters and inspection. Liberty party ashore.

15th, Monday. Overcast and cloudy to partly cloudy and hazy. At anchor, Santa Cruz, underway for and at anchor off Mare Island, Cal. At 7.56 got underway, leading Second Division, in column, natural order, distance 500 yards, speed 15 knots, and sailed for Mare Island. At 12.40 entered the Golden Gate and headed for Vallejo. Sighted West Virginia and Maryland leaving Carquines Straits for Mare Island Navy Yard. Anchored off Mare Island at 2.50 p. m. Commanding Officers of Washington, California and South Dakota called on board. At 5.30 p. m. South Dakota shifted anchorage. Liberty party ashore.

16th, Tuesday. Partly cloudy and pleasant. At anchor off Mare Island. Water barge came alongside. Commanding Officer of Maryland called. The Commanding Officer, California, Commandant and Captain Mare Island Navy Yard, and Commander of Second Torpedo Flotilla called on board. California sailed for San Francisco to go into dry dock. Steamer Fruto came alongside to deliver stores. Liberty party ashore.

17th, Wednesday. Partly cloudy and pleasant. At anchor off Mare Island, Cal. South Dakota coaling. Commander, Second Division and Commanding Officer left to make official calls. Commanding Officers of Perry and Farragut called on board. Lieutenant-Commander F. H. Clark, Jr., U. S. Navy, reported on board for duty as Navigating Officer, under orders from Navy Department. Baseball and liberty party ashore.

18th, Thursday. Clear and pleasant. At anchor off Mare Island. Lieut.-Commander S. S. Robison, U. S. N., was detached from duty as Navigator and ordered to the Pennsylvania as Executive Officer, under orders from Navy Department. Commander, Second Division, left ship and hauled down flag. A. N. Williams, yeoman, 1st class, reported on board from Pensacola.

19th, Friday. At anchor, off Mare Island, underway for and at anchor off San Francisco. Partly cloudy and cool. Got underway at 5.35 p. m., proceeded to San Francisco and anchored at 8.41 p. m. off Union Iron Works.

20th, Saturday. Overcast, misty and drizzling. At anchor, San Francisco. At 8.00 a. m. saluted Commander-in-Chief, Atlantic Fleet, with 13 guns; returned with 7. Assistant Naval Constructor L. B. McBride reported on board for duty in connection with docking. Commander, Second Division, returned on board and hoisted his flag. Georgia entered harbor and saluted Commander-in-Chief, Atlantic Fleet, with 13 guns. At 3.30 p. m. Tug Sea Queen came alongside to assist in docking. At 4.32 p. m. got nnderway, and entered dry-dock at Hunter's Point at 5.32 p. m., resting on blocks at 5.44 p. m. Crew engaged in scraping bottom.

21st, Sunday. In dry-dock, Hunter's Point. Partly cloudy and pleasant. Scraping ship's bottom, painting same and renewing zincs.

22nd, Monday.—In dry-dock and at anchor, San Francisco. Fair and pleasant; slightly hazy. Crew engaged in painting bottom, renewing zincs, regrinding valves, etc. At 5.35 p. m. flooded dock and ship floated. At 6.30 p. m. Tug Sea Queen took stern line to assist in undocking. At 6.35 p. m. got underway and anchored in harbor at 7.28 p. m. Found First Division of Atlantic Fleet; also, Georgia, Louisiana and California at anchor.

23rd, Tuesday. Clear and pleasant. At anchor, San Francisco. Collier Fitzpatrick came alongside 5.30 a. m. Coaling ship. California sailed for Mare Island. Illinois came in and anchored. Captain T. B. Howard detached from Tennessee. Read orders at muster.

24th, Wednesday. Clear and fine. Finished coaling 10 a. m.; took 1422 tons. Ensign B. Dutton, U. S. N., reported on board for duty under orders from Navy Department. Preble sailed for Mare Island at 3.20 p.m. Half masted colors in memory of ex-President Cleveland.

25th, Thursday. Partly cloudy and pleasant. At anchor, San Francisco. Half masted colors for ex-President Cleveland, colors to be half masted until July 25th. Naval Constructor S. M. Henry reported on board for duty on practice cruise to San Diego.

26th, Friday. Partly cloudy, warm and pleasant. At anchor, San Francisco. New Jersey came in and anchored at 6.15 a. m. At 10.15 a. m. Commander Second Division left ship and hoisted his flag on U. S. S. Preble and sailed for Mare Island. Washington came in and anchored at 2.33 p. m. Fired gun each half-hour in memory of ex-President Cleveland. Commander Second Division returned on board and hoisted his flag at 5.15 p. m.

27th, Saturday. Fair and pleasant. Washington docked at Hunter's Point at 11 a. m. California came in and anchored at 4 p. m. Midshipman H. R. Keller detached and ordered to Farragut. Second Lieut. C. P. Meyer, U. S. M. C., detached and ordered to Kearsarge. H. H. Melchert, ordinary seaman, received from New Jersey.

28th, Sunday. Fair and warm. At anchor, San Francisco. Nebraska came in and anchored at 7.10 p. m. Held divine service. W. C. Humphrey, ordinary seaman, transferred to New Jersey.

29th, Monday. Fair and pleasant. At anchor, San Francisco. Preble and Perry came in and anchored. Gunner J. F. McCarthy detached and ordered to Kentucky.

30th, Tuesday. At anchor, San Francisco. Partly cloudy and pleasant.

★ ★ ★

THE BASE BALL WORLD

A series of games to decide the championship of the teams of the Second Division, U. S. Pacific Fleet, was arranged and partly played off during the month of June.

The Tennessee's team at present occupies a favorable position in the standing, and if past perfermances are even equalled, will have no trouble in carrying off first honors in the Second Division.

Our team has played the following games since June 1st: June 2—Tennessee, 19; California, 13. June 29—Tennessee, 10; California, 13.

The following is the standing of the Second Division teams at the end of June:

	G	W	L	Pct.
California....	6	4	2	.666
Washington .	6	4	2	.666
Tennessee ...	2	1	1	.500
South Dakota	4	0	4	.000

★ ★ ★

An Open-Face Watch

In the Swim

Whose Goat?

Mr. Used to be—I was a confounded fool when I entered this Navy.
On the job—It has not changed you any, I see.

* * *

Takes a drop—The thermometer, the price of eggs, and J. M.

* * *

Wireless, harmless, sporty gent,
Had his nails polished for 50 cents.
If he spent that 50 cents for brains
He wouldn't have his nails polished again.

* * *

A great many things are done in the name of charity; and bluejackets too.

* * *

The sweet music teacher from Venice—Really, I just dote on Chopin.
Larkin—Yes, but the stores must be crowded now.

* * *

Life at the Presidio is so military, they even drill wells.

* * *

IN FRISCO: Bluejacket—Rates please.
Hotel Clerk—$3 up.
Bluejacket—But I am a robber.
Clerk—What has that to do with it?
Bluejacket—I thought you might recognize the profession.

* * *

Looking over the muster roll we find Smith, Smythe, Smithe, Schmidt, Schmid and Smyth. The Lord bless poor old John.

* * *

Money isn't everything—for instance $5 in a prohibition town.

The farm for mine, said Stein, and if it does not rain I will plant onions with the potatoes, causing their eyes to smart, and thus save myself the trouble of carrying water.

* * *

Bluejacket, wandering into church—How long has the minister been preaching?

Sexton—Some 30 years, young man.

Bluejacket—It is hardly worth while to wait, as he must be nearly through now.

* * *

Since we visited Redondo and other California ports,
Our whole ship seems to be upset; we have all kinds of sports,
The Fourth division is the winner, by the latest kind of dope
And they keep the canteen busy serving out the fancy soap,
Almond cream and pretty gill guys, they buy all such stuff as that,
And the next thing that we look for is the Merry Widow hat.
That old saying is a true one, even with the boys in blue,
If beauty's skin deep we advise you, see the barber, he'll skin you.
Some of you are really pretty, but for many there's no hope,
If you would be a Beau Brummell, please buy something more than soap.

★ ★ ★

ITINERARY—U. S. S. TENNESSEE

Port	Arrival	Departure	Miles
League Island, Pa. (com's'd).	July 17, '06	Nov. 1, '06	233
Hampton Roads, Va.	Nov. 3	8	98
Piney Point, Md.	8	8	1834
Colon, Panama	14	15	130
Chiriqui Lagoon	16	16	1041
Ponce, Porto Rico	21	22	1285
Hampton Roads, Va.	26	Dec. 16	240
League Island, Pa.	Dec. 18	Apr. 12, '07	233
Hampton Roads, Va.	Apr. 13, '07	14	15
Lynn Haven Bay, Va.	14	16	16
Hampton Roads, Va	16	May 16	530
Provincetown, Mass.	May 18	24	53
Boston, Mass.	25	June 5	555
Hampton Roads, Va	June 7	11	382
Newport, R. I.	12	14	3112
Royan, France	23	July 2	52
Ile D' Aix, France	July 2	3	10

Port	Arrival	Departure	Miles
La Rochelle, France	3	11	235
Brest, France	12	25	3194
Tompkinsville, S. I.	Aug. 6	Aug. 16	270
Hampton Roads, Va.	17	17	392
Newport, R. I.	18	19	265
Boston, Mass	20	Sept. 30	265
Newport, R. I.	Oct. 1	Oct. 4	392
Hampton Roads, Va	5	12	1904
Port of Spain, Trinidad	18	24	3300
Rio de Janeiro, Brazil	Nov. 4	Nov. 10	1044
Montevideo, Uruguay	13	19	1325
Punta Arenas, Chile	23	27	2760
Callao, Peru	Dec. 5	Dec. 12	2240
Acapulco, Mexico	19	22	785
Pichilinque Bay, Mexico	25	28	315
Magdalena Bay, Mexico	29	Feb. 15, '08	1026
San Francisco, Cal	Feb. 20, '08	29	287
Santa Barbara, Cal	Mar. 1	Mar. 6	164
San Diego, Cal	6	16	96
San Pedro, Cal	16	23	18
Redondo, Cal	23	25	9
Venice, Cal	25	27	275
Monterey, Cal	28	29	92
San Francisco, Cal	29	Apr. 1	738
Port Angeles, Wash	Apr. 4	6	36
Port Townsend, Wash	6	8	45
Bellingham, Wash	8	11	32
Blaine, Wash	11	12	87
Everett, Wash	12	13	30
Seattle, Wash	13	17	22
Tacoma, Wash	17	19	26
Puget Sound, Navy Yard	19	May 1	840
San Francisco, Cal	May 4	17	287
Santa Barbara, Cal	18	22	82
San Pedro, Cal	22	25	82
Santa Barbara, Cal	25	28	82
San Pedro, Cal	29	30	28
Venice, Cal	29	June 1	67
Santa Barbara	June 1	5	82
San Pedro	5	12	82
Santa Barbara	13	13	228
Santa Cruz	14	15	91
Carquines Straits	15	25	29
San Francisco	25	....	....

Book Seven

The Volunteer

August 1908

Published Monthly
On Board the
U. S. S. Tennessee

No. 5688-404   NAVY DEPARTMENT,
                    WASHINGTON, JULY 9, 1908.

SIR:—

1. The Department takes pleasure in informing you that at the annual record target practice of 1908 the vessel under your command attained a final merit of more than eighty-five per cent of the final merit of the winning vessel of her class.

2. The Department congratulates you and the officers and men under your command and commends the intelligent and zealous training which has produced this gratifying degree of efficiency.

3. You will please publish this letter at general muster.

                    Very respectfully,
                        (Sgd.) J. E. Pillsbury,
                                    Acting Secretary.

The Commanding Officer,
      U. S. S. Tennessee.

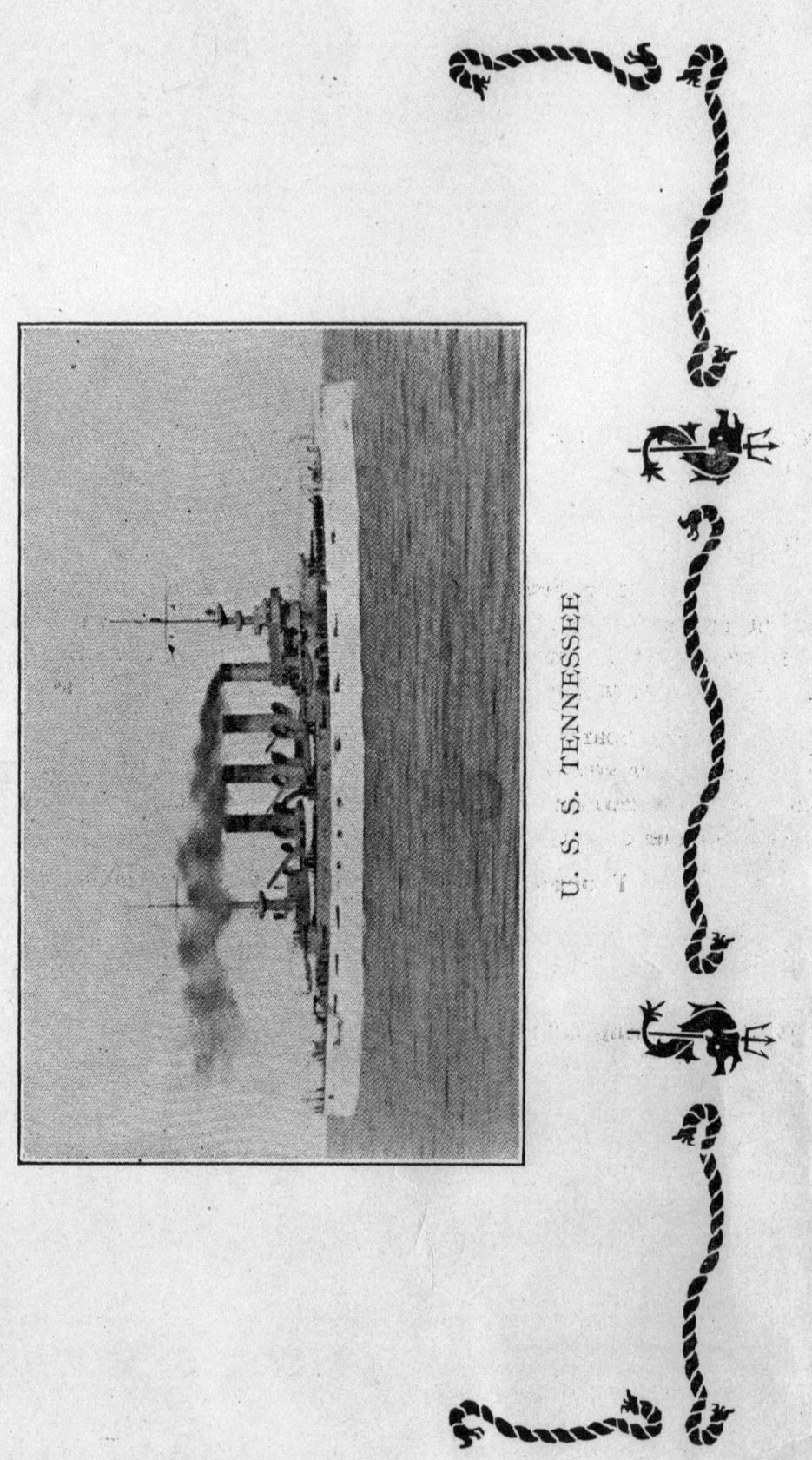

U. S. S. TENNESSEE

THE VOLUNTEER
For : August : 1908

OUR CRUISE

THE Second Division, U. S. Pacific Fleet, together with the torpedo boat destroyers Preble, Perry and Farragut, having received orders to conduct an experimental towing cruise from San Francisco, Cal., to San Diego, Cal., and return, the Squadron got underway on July 1st, at 10 a. m., and left the harbor of San Francisco. Shortly after passing through the Golden Gate, each cruiser took a torpedo boat in tow, the Tennessee towing the Preble, the Washington the Perry, and the California the Farragut. Heading towards San Diego, we proceeeed at about ten knots speed, in moderate weather, and after a pleasant trip, anchored off Coronado Beach at 5 p. m. on July 3rd. As this anchorage is not ideal for smaller vessels, the torpedo craft steamed inside the harbor of San Diego.

The glorious old Fourth, the favorite holiday with the man-of-warsman, was celebrated in the customary style, by full dressing ship at colors and firing the national salute of 21 guns at noon. A baseball game between the teams of the Tennessee and California was arranged and played in the afternoon, the Tennessee winning. Pay-day occurred on the 3rd and generous liberty was granted and thoroughly enjoyed in San Diego and the surrounding country.

At the last record practice, the U. S. S. Preble failed to retain the torpedo trophy for excellent markmanship and was forced to transfer the much esteemed token to the Perry. The little vessels steamed out to the flagship and amid appropriate ceremonies the trophy was transferred, a salute being fired in honor of the occasion.

After a stay of approximately four days at Coronado, the vessels again got underway for San Francisco, this time the California and Tennessee changing tows. The run up the coast was ideal and the sea like glass a good part of the voyage. The Squadron anchored off Folsom street, in San Francisco harbor, at 9.15 a. m. on the 9th.

Shortly after the arrival of the Tennessee, Captain Bradley A. Fiske, U. S. Navy, our new commanding officer, reported on board and assumed command, Lieutenant-Commander Field having been in command since the departure of Captain Howard on the 23rd of June.

The vessels of the Second Division having been ordered to the navy yards for minor repairs and the installation of fire control systems, the California left the anchorage and proceeded to Mare Island on the 10th; also the torpedo boats. The Tennessee left for California City on the 10th and coaled on the 11th, taking on board 535 tons, returning to the anchorage that night.

On July 12th, the Tennessee left the harbor, in company with the Washington, and headed up the coast for Puget Sound. The trip up was beautiful, the weather being pleasant and the sea smooth during the entire trip. Shortly after passing through the Golden Gate the Pacific Mail Steamer Governor was picked up and remained on the starboard hand until after the vessels rounded Cape Flattery, when the Tennessee and Washington increased the speed, the Governor gradually fading away. A contagious disease having occurred on the Washington, that vessel left the formation and proceeded to Port Townsend, the Tennessee continuing to the Puget Sound Navy Yard and anchoring at 8 p. m. off the Navy Yard. The Charleston, flying the flag of Rear Admiral W. T. Swinburne, was at the dock; also the Colorado and Pennsylvania. The St. Louis was also anchored in the stream.

This completed the cruising for July, the Tennessee remaining at the dock for the balance of the month.

CHANGES FOR JULY, 1908

TRANSFERRED.—F. A. Varalla, Bandmaster, to Franklin, Norfolk, Va.; R. Logan, fireman, 2nd class, to Mare Island Hospital, Cal.; K. Lawrence, ordinary seaman, to Hospital, Bremerton, Wash.

RATINGS.—D. Smith, Gunnery Sergeant, to 1st Sergeant; F. Geppel, Musician 1st class, to 1st Musician; J. F. Netzel, Painter, 3rd class, to coal passer.

RECEIVED.—G. J. Eicher, Yeoman, 1st class, from Independence, July 26.

DISCHARGED.—J. J. Mohan, Boatswain's Mate, 1st class, July 6; H. R. Clark, Shipwright, July 10; P. H. Kelly, Water-tender, July 11; M. F. Gluth, Coxswain, July 26.

ENLISTMENT.—C. D. Olds, Jr., coal passer, at San Diego, Cal., July 6.

★ ★ ★

ON THE FORECASTLE

The little hand I pressed, ah, me!
That I but pressed and did depart,
How tenderly I think of thee;
I wonder fondly where thou art.

I wonder whether thou shalt e'er
Feel once again my tender clasp.
With thee the world and all were mine,
I saw the prize within my grasp.

The little hand I pressed, ah, me!
And held with all the lover's art,
A royal flush—and "Legs" showed up,
He grabbed the pot and did depart.

★ ★ ★

Why are the yeomen almost like ball players? They hate to be put out; also, like to get home without being touched.

An electrician has purchased a new suit of loose fitting B. V. D.'s. Anybody wishing to view his stately shape may do so by lingering in the vicinity of the dynamo room, or in the central passage, where he makes his appearance at reveille and six bells.

Gunner's Gang, U. S. S. Tennessee

Table of Approximate Distances

	Panama	Acapulco	Pichilinque	Magdalena Bay	San Diego	San Pedro	Santa Barbara	San Francisco	Portland	Astoria	Tatoosh	Seattle	Vancouver
Victoria	4115	2616	2098	1796	1206	1122	1045	773	313	216	64	90	96
Vancouver	4180	2681	2168	1861	1271	1187	1110	848	388	291	139	126	
Seattle	4165	2666	2148	1846	1256	1172	1095	833	373	276	124		
Tatoosh	4040	2542	2024	1722	1132	1048	971	709	249	152			
Astoria	4000	2504	1986	1684	1094	920	843	581	97				
Portland	4010	2511	1993	1691	1101	1017	940	678					
San Francisco	3360	1863	1345	1043	453	369	292						
Santa Barbara	3080	1583	1065	763	173	89							
San Pedro	3000	1494	976	674	94								
San Diego	2930	1430	912	610									
Magdalena Bay	2340	840	327										
Pichilinque	1425	770											
Acapulco	1500												

San Francisco to Honolulu....2100 Miles
Honolulu to Samoa............2263 Miles
Honolulu to San Diego........2122 Miles

THE VOLUNTEER

PUBLISHED MONTHLY ABOARD THE U. S. S. TENNESSEE

J. E. ERWIN................................PUBLISHER

VOL. 1 NO. 7.   PRICE, 15 CENTS

Navy Yard, Puget Sound, August, 1908

¶ A remarkable contrast to the fine fleet reviewed by the Secretary of the Navy in San Francisco harbor in May last, is the U. S. S. Essex, our first American warship to enter the Pacific.

First Warship in Pacific

The Essex turned Cape Horn, flying the stars and stripes on January 26, 1813, and entered the Western Ocean, with one poor chart of the Pacific aboard, and a determination among officers and men to provision the ship at the expense of the enemy. Then the second war with Great Britain was raging. ¶ The cruise of the Essex was vastly different from that of the squadron of today. The Essex missed meeting the Squadron of Commodore Bainbridge in the Carribean Sea, as planned. British ships started in pursuit of the lone Essex, and rather than seek refuge in any of the Atlantic ports of South America, Captain David Porter determined to turn Cape Horn and enter the Pacific. ¶ The arrival of the Essex in the Pacific was timely. Chili had just declared her independence of Spain. The viceroy of Peru was sending out privateers to prey on U. S. ships. The Essex taught the South Americans to respect the star spangled banner.

The Essex also wiped British commerce from the Pacific Ocean, along the South American coast, doing to England a damage of $6,000,000, a big sum for the time. The Essex also equipped and provisioned herself at the expense of the enemy for a year. The British were alarmed at the work of the Essex, and sent ships of war to catch her, fitting out the Phoebe, in particular, with long range guns, so that she might destroy the Essex from a safe distance and not get into the deadly range of the smaller guns of the Essex. ¶ The Phoebe and the Cherub attacked and defeated the Essex in the harbor of Valpariso in February, 1814. They had seventeen long guns, firing 288 pounds of metal, to the six long guns throwing only 66 pounds of metal on the Essex, and 500 men to 250 on the Essex. ¶ Captain Porter had asked for heavier guns, but the Department in Washington had refused them. The Essex maintained the unequal fight with splendid heroism for several hours. She surrendered when there was fit for service but one officer besides Captain Porter and 75 men. ¶ The Essex was built on Winter Island, Salem, of Essex oak, and by Essex men. It was a gift of merchants of Salem and others to the government. The vessel was launched September 30, 1799. She became a deep sea sailor and fighter and made history as did many of the brave old wooden ships. Admiral Farragut and many other gallant sailors served on her.

★ ★ ★

COMPLETION OF VESSELS, JULY 1

The following was the degree of completion on July 1, of vessels under construction for the United States Navy: Battleships—South Carolina, 51.9; Michigan, 57.2; Delaware, 31.6; North Dakota, 40.5. Armored cruisers — Montana, 99.2*. Scout cruisers—Salem, 98.9. Torpedoboat destroyers—No. 17, 31.1; No. 18, 26.9; No. 19, 33.8; No. 20, 13; No. 21, 13. Submarine torpedoboats—No. 13, 49.3; No. 14, 49.4; No. 15, 48.6; No. 16, 48.8; No. 17, 35.8; No. 18, 32.6; No. 19, 31.7. Colliers—Vestal, 89.1; Prometheus, 66.8. Tugboats—Patapsco, 75; Patuxent, 72.2. *Delivered at navy yard, Norfolk, July 10.

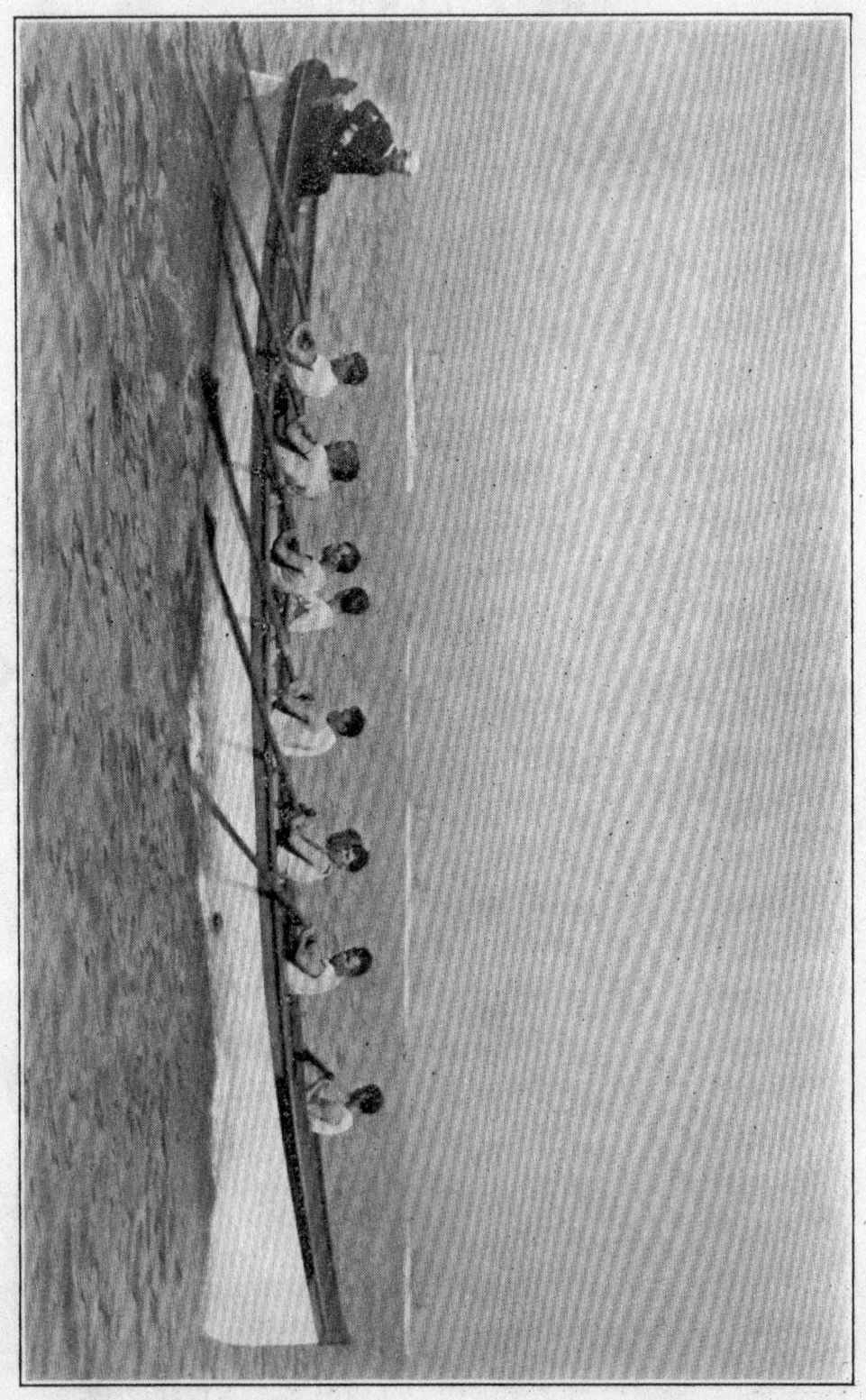

Race-boat Crew, U. S. S. Tennessee

FRYE'S DREAM

We rounded Flattery in a gale,
The sea piled mountains high,
I was the lookout out on the truck,
No sun shown in the sky,
The waves crashed madly against the ship
As through the foam we sped;
I gazed into the thickness,
There was something dead ahead.

A mighty ship, as sure as life,
Or something large and strong,
My voice seemed frozen to my throat,
Our ship steamed madly on
To unutterable destruction
In this cruel, angry sea,
And a general court-martial,
Perhaps death, awaited me.

I tried my best to speak a word
Fate held me in its grasp;
"For God's sake, Captain, stop the ship,"
I bellowed out at last,
"Well done, my boy," the Captain said,
"You are the nation's pride."
The helm went hard a starboard—
And a steamer grazed our side.

Next morning on the quarter-deck,
With all hands mustered aft
The Captain told the thrilling tale
That nearly sunk our craft.
"A Boatswain, lad, you'll surely be
For avoiding such a wreck."
But my hammock lashing parted—
And I landed on the deck.

Just Gossip

Absent-mindedly a bluejacket yawned. Pardon me he said, I did not mean it. "I see," responded the would-be Navy mail clerk, "opened by mistake."

Overtime from liberty; what have you to say, asked the Captain. I hurried for the boat but slipped on a banana peel and sprained my knee, replied the delinquent. Captain: Lame excuse; fourth class.

Well sir, recently said a petty officer of the Tennessee to his prospective father-in-law, when I marry your daughter I expect everything will run like clock work. Yes, said the father, tick, tick.

Say shipmate, lend me a dollar for a week, old man. The sailor: Who is the weak old man?

The Frisco Panhandler: Please give me ten cents for a bed. Pat Soffen: Bring the bed around, I'll take a look at it.

Recruit: Sir, I have a splinter in my hand. Doctor: What have you been doing, stroking your head?

A Bremerton youth wandering about the deck was asked if he wished to enlist. I would sooner be in a lunatic asylum said the youth, No doubt you would be more at home, said sinful Charlie, of the first division.

Tallapoosa: I tell you, mate, the men of today are not what they used to be. Modern Sailor: No, they were children once.

A bright little visitor at Bremerton: Mamma, did that sailor shoot anybody? Mamma: Child, why do you ask such a question? Little One: The other man said he was loaded.

He was an untried sportsman, but was in for the race-boat's crew: I want two pair of rowing pants, said he—those with the sliding seat.

They tell me this outside life is a tough proposition; but, if I cannot make it go it is back to the recruiting office and if I am turned down I'll hang myself to the lamp post in front. One who has just shipped: There is a sign there says "No hanging around here."

ON THE DIAMOND

During the month of July, a great deal of progress has been made in deciding the championship of the Second Division, and our team has held its own in good shape.

The following unofficial games were played with teams from other vessels:

Tennessee, 17; Colorado, 3.   Tennessee, 10; Charleston, 3.

Games which count in the series for the championship follow:

July 6—Tennessee, 8; California, 3.   July 25—Tennessee, 2; Washington, 1.   July 29—Washington, 5; Tennessee, 1.

STANDING OF CLUBS.

Team	Played	Won	Lost	Pct.
California	9	6	3	.666
Washington	8	5	3	.625
Tennessee	5	3	2	.600
South Dakota	6	0	6	.000

At the time of going to press, the Tennessee has one game to play with the Washington and three with the South Dakota, and, by winning these, will carry off the championship of the Division.

The gunner's mates, having received the idea from some source or other that they could play ball, challenged the yeomen to a game, which was played on July 22, resulting in a score of 18 to 5 in favor of the yeomen. The features of the game are too numerous to receive just consideration, but the game was well played (by the yeomen) and was very interesting from start to finish.

Line-up—Yeomen: Russel, c; Williams, p; Wallace, 1b; Thomas, 2b; Cash, 3b; Gumbiner, ss; Wirth, rf; Evans, cf; Massey, lf. Gunner's Mates: Robinson, c; Finnerty, p; Walling, 1b; Murray, 2b; Langfield, 3b; Rodarte, ss; Chandler, rf; Costello, cf; Heim, lf.   Umpire, Bugler Meeghan.

SMALL ARMS PRACTICE

The second and fourth companies went to American Lake, located about 14 miles from Tacoma, on the Northern Pacific Railway, to have small arms practice. They embarked on the Tug Navajo on Tuesday, the 21st, and went to Tacoma, thence via rail to within about one and one-half miles from the camp, the balance of the journey being made on foot. Camping conditions were excellent, there being an unlimited supply of fresh water and many other conveniences not found at many ranges. The party returned on Thursday, the 30th, and everyone reported a fine time. Lieutenant W. L. Pryor had charge, assisted by Ensign Olding and Midshipmen Baker and Gross. Following is a list of those composing the party:

Gowan, BM2c
Mergans, Cox
Sullivan, D, Act Cox
McGrath, D, os
Tunney, T, os
Peterson, C B, os
McCafferty, J, os
Bundy, N F, sea
McQuillen, W, os
Burch, B W, os
Shackleton, W R, os
Wilson, C E, os
Myers, F S, os
Young, D L, os
Larkin, J T, sea
Devlin, W H, os
Reuter, G L, os
Sherrie, os
Speicher, M J, os
Ward, T J, os
Weisus, P A, os
Wivagg, E O, os
Thomas, J, os
Ishler, W Y, os
Baker, L J, os
Swiatecki, J K, os
Workman, H M, os
Madison, J V, BM2c
McCabe, W E, sea
Malinowski, W, os
From, E G, os
Olsen, S, os
Lechler, W H, sea
Whipple, E C, os
Hicks, C E, sea
Ritz, C, os
Houghton, R B, os
Lene, B J, os
Wenegi, os
Warner, S, os
Potter, S P, os
Lawler, J F, os
Neibich, H G, os
Lecklider, E A, os
Wytaske, P, sea
Butler, J T, os
Nickerson, H N, os
Shoemaker, B L, os
Critchfield, W, os
Doyle, W, os
Snyder, L A, os
Kirk, J H, os
Wright, G E, os
Rey, H E, os
Krause, F, BM2c
Vortriede, H, BM2c
Breslin, G, Cox
Kelly, M W, Cox
Sanford, O C, Cox
Noethen, E, sea

U. S. S. Tennessee Band

Welsh, J L, os
Cerbin, A, os
Russell, C D, os
Pritchard, C, os
O'Neil, H A, os
Nickerson, H M, os
Milliken, R D, os
Warnick, N W, os
Miller, F J, sea
Schierlch, S L, os
Youell, R, os
Natter, J, os
Wooten, G, os
Rhoades, D L, os
Seiber, J O, os
Taft, P H, os
Oder, R J, os
Warner, W F, os
House, G G, os
Bennett, J W, os
Steif, C H, os
Kemper, C, os
Lynch, C V, os
Marshburn, W V, os
Bagley, J A, sea
Maloney, H T, os
Melchoir, E G, os
Cramer, F, sea
Mahan, D L, os

Williams, C H, os
Ripley, F W, os
Moffitt, W, os
Pheasey, H, sea
Mendenhall, E A, os
Wollner, E G, os
Monroe, F, os
Hunter, G, sea
Thomas, E A, os
Taylor, V A, os
Bradley, C E, os
Myers, G E, os
Morgan, D G, os
Sutor, F, os
Stoffell, W A, os
Lear, L Z, os
Marberry, E R, os
Weidner, L M, os
Cunningham, F E, os
Garren, W X, CM1c
Northup, N M, Elec
Austin, G, CGM
Boyker, E D, HApp1c
Wise, J H, MAtt
Fritz, SC
Schlereth, W B, SC
Zurlinden, W, Bug
Pierce, F B, HApp1c

Little drops of water, little grains of sand,
Show the sailing party has been upon the land.

Meeghan, the Umpire

With padded breast and nerve of steel
He sauntered forth upon the field,
The inkslingers before him crawl,
With thundrous roar he yells "Play Ball!"

DAILY LOG FOR JULY, 1908

1st, Wednesday. Overcast and misty to partly cloudy and cool. At anchor, San Francisco; at sea, enroute for San Diego, Cal. Nebraska and New Jersey coaling. Virginia came in and anchored at 11.10 a. m. R. R. Rice, blacksmith, transferred to Independence for temporary duty. Preble made fast astern, then shoved off and anchored. At 1 p. m. Tennessee, Washington, California, Preble, Perry and Farragut got underway and left the harbor. After passing over bar took Preble in tow, Washington took Perry and California took Farragut, steaming to Southward for experimental cruise. Midshipman H. B. Labhardt reported on board for duty. At 10.38 p. m. tow line parted and Preble continued under own steam. Washington and California also lost tows.

2nd, Thursday. Overcast, cloudy and misty, with occasional rain. At sea, enroute to San Diego, Cal. Took Preble in tow at 5 a. m. Running at various speeds for experimental purposes. Passed Point Arguello at 5.50 p. m.

3rd, Friday. Fair and pleasant. At sea, enroute for San Diego, and at anchor off Coronado Beach, Cal. Passed two steamers and a sailing vessel. Sighted high land at 3.56 p. m. At 5 p. m. cast off Preble and anchored off Coronado Beach, with Washington and California. The Preble, Perry and Farragut steamed into San Diego harbor and anchored.

4th, Saturday. At anchor off Coronado Beach, Cal. Partly cloudy, fair and warm. Full dressed ship at 8 a. m. Sent liberty party ashore at 10 a. m. Ship open to visitors; large number on board. At 12 noon all men-of-war present fired national salute of 21 guns. Sent baseball party ashore to play California. Commanding Officer of Fort Rosecrans, Commanding Officers Washington, California, Preble, Perry and Farragut called officially on board.

5th, Sunday. Fair and pleasant. At anchor, off Coronado Beach. At 9.15 a. m. U. S. S. Alert passed in to San Diego. At 9.20 a. m. Italian man-of-war Pulgia steamed in from Southward and fired 15-gun salute with American flag at fore. Salute returned gun for gun by Tennessee and Fort Rosecrans.

Liberty party ashore. Sailing parties out. Visitors on board. Held divine service.

6th, Monday. Fair and pleasant. At anchor off Coronado Beach. Exercised at routine drills. Sent fire and rescue party around Washington. At 2 p. m. Second Torpedo Flotilla came out and anchored off port quarter. Preble fired salute of 21 guns and hauled down trophy pennant. At 3.20 p. m. Perry broke trophy pennant and Tennessee saluted with 21 guns. Division Commander and Commanding Officer left ship to attend ceremonies of transfer. At 3.17 p. m. Farragut made fast astern. At 3.25 p. m. Preble and Perry got underway and went into San Diego. At 4.10 p. m. Farragut cast off and left for San Diego. J. J. Mohan, boatswain's mate, 1st class, honorably discharged, enlistment having expired. At 5 p. m. Italian man-of-war Pulgia fired salute of 13 guns, returned by Tennessee. Liberty and baseball parties ashore.

7th, Tuesday. Partly cloudy and pleasant. At anchor off Coronado and at sea, enroute to San Francisco, Cal. Naval Constructor Henry left ship and went to Farragut for trip North. At 10 a. m. got underway and took Farragut in tow at 10.42, steaming Northward, Washington with Perry in tow and California towing Preble. Passed three steamers.

8th, Wednesday. Cloudy and overcast, clearing at end. At sea, enroute to San Francisco, Cal. At 1.10 p. m. passed Santa Cruz light; also steamer standing south. At 1.53 p. m. tow line parted, picked up again at 2.15 and went ahead, continuing throughout day.

9th, Thursday. Overcast and hazy first part, then pleasant. At sea, enroute to San Francisco and at anchor in San Francisco harbor. At 5.40 a. m. Farragut cast off. At 6.45 sighted San Francisco Lightship. Steamed into San Francisco harbor and anchored at 9.23 a. m. St. Louis in port. Commanding Officers of St. Louis and Pensacola called officially. Assistant Naval Constructor Henry reported on board from Farragut. Pensacola saluted flag of Division Commander with 13 guns, returned with 7 guns. Preble, Perry and Farragut sailed for Mare Island. Captain Bradley A. Fiske reported on board and took command. Got underway at 4.50

Some of the Fifth Division, U. S. S. Tennessee

p. m., steamed to California City and anchored at 6.00 p. m.

10th, Friday. Fair and pleasant. At anchor off California City, enroute for and at anchor off San Francisco. Finished coaling ship, taking on board 532 tons. Got underway at 5 p. m. and anchored in San Francisco harbor at 6.00 p. m. Transferred R. Logan, fireman, second class, to Naval Hospital, Mare Island, and F. A. Varalla, bandmaster, to Franklin, at Norfolk, Va.

11th, Saturday. Partly cloudy and pleasant. At anchor, San Francisco. Taking stores from tug Herald. Received 49 men for transfer to the Nipsic on arrival at Puget Sound.

12th, Sunday. Partly cloudy to overcast and misty. At anchor, San Francisco, Cal., and at sea, enroute to Navy Yard, Puget Sound, Wash. Got underway at 1.30 p. m., and stood out of harbor in natural order with Washington, distance 500 yards. Had Sunday quarters and inspection of ship and crew. Passed three steamers and several sailing vessels.

13th, Monday. At sea, enroute to Puget Sound Navy Yard. Overcast and cloudy first part, then clearing and pleasant. In column, open order, 500 yards distant. Passed several sailing ships and steamers.

14th, Tuesday. Partly cloudy and pleasant. At sea, enroute for Puget Sound Navy Yard and at anchor off Puget Sound Navy Yard. At 11.21 a. m. rounded Cape Flattery and stood in for Puget Sound. At 1.12 p. m. sheered to starboard and communicated with British ship Lonsdale, which was displaying distress signals, but did not require assistance. At 5.40 p. m. Washington left formation and went into Port Townsend to go into quarantine, a contagious disease having been discovered. Steamed into Puget Sound and anchored off Navy Yard at 7.36 p. m. Transferred 49 passengers to Nipsic. Milwaukee, St. Louis, Charleston, Colorado and Pennsylvania in port.

15th, Wednesday. Partly cloudy and pleasant first part, then overcast and drizzling. At anchor off Puget Sound Navy Yard and moored to dock. Official calls exchanged with Navy Yard officials. Commander, Second Division, hauled down his flag at 8.05 a. m. At 12.05 p. m. Washington came in and anchored, flying quarantine flag. Washington saluted the Commandant with 13 guns; returned by yard battery with 7 guns. Sent funeral party ashore to attend funeral services of member of crew of Washington. At 5.22 p. m. got underway, assisted by tug, and moored to dock at 6.00 p. m. Sent liberty party ashore.

16th, Thursday. Overcast, hazy and misty. Moored to dock, Puget Sound Navy Yard. Rear Admiral Swinburne, Commanding Second Squadron, Pacific Fleet, and the Commanding Officers of the Pennsylvania and Colorado called officially. Sent liberty party ashore.

17th, Friday. Partly cloudy and pleasant; warm. Moored to dock, Navy Yard. Sent liberty party ashore.

18th, Saturday. Fair and pleasant; warm. Moored to dock, Navy Yard. At 10.38 a. m. Rear Admiral W. T. Burwell hauled down his flag upon his retirement; yard battery saluted with 13 guns; also saluted flag of Rear Admiral Swinburne with 13 guns. Captain J. A. Rodgers hoisted his pennant as Commandant of the Yard and was saluted by St. Louis with 7 guns. Yard workmen aboard. Commander, Second Division, called officially on Pennsylvania, Colorado and Charleston. Commandant of Navy Yard called on board. Liberty and baseball parties ashore. Commander, Second Division, hauled down his flag at 5.06 p. m.

19th, Sunday. Fair and pleasant; warm. Mustered at Sunday quarters and had inspection of ship and crew. Liberty, baseball, visiting and sailing parties. Visitors aboard.

20th, Monday. Fair and pleasant; warm. Moored to dock, Navy Yard. Commander, Second Division, returned on board and hoisted flag; called on Commandant of Navy Yard. Charleston shifted berth. Washington came out of quarantine.

21st, Tuesday. Partly cloudy and warm. Moored to dock, Navy Yard. At 5.00 a. m. Washington got underway and moored to dock. At 11 a. m. 2nd and 4th companies left on Tug Navajo for rifle range at American Lake to conduct small arms practice. Crew engaged in painting upper works. Yard workmen aboard. Taking on stores from yard. Baseball and liberty parties ashore.

22nd, Wednesday. Partly cloudy and hazy. Moored to dock, Navy Yard. At 7.30 a. m. Pennsylvania sent rifle team out. Baseball and liberty party ashore. Yard workmen on board.

23rd, Thursday. Cloudy, hazy and warm. Moored to dock, Navy Yard. Crew engaged in painting ship. Yard workmen on board. Sent baseball and liberty parties ashore.

24th, Friday. Partly cloudy and warm to overcast and rainy last part. Moored to dock, Navy Yard. Yard workmen on board. Baseball and liberty parties ashore.

25th, Saturday. Partly cloudy and warm. K. Lawrence, ordinary seaman, transferred to Naval Hospital, Puget Sound Navy Yard. Yard workmen on board. Baseball and liberty parties ashore. Baseball team defeated Washington's team by score of 2-1.

26th, Sunday. Fair and pleasant. Moored to dock, Navy Yard. Mustered at quarters for inspection. Published articles for Government of the Navy. Sent baseball, handball and liberty parties ashore. M. F. Gluth, coxswain, honorably discharged. Asst. Surgeon J. B. Kaufman left ship to join party at rifle range.

27th, Monday. Partly cloudy and pleasant. Moored to dock, Navy Yard. Commander, Second Squadron, Pacific Fleet, hauled down his flag and left the Charleston to join the West Virginia for duty as Commander-in-Chief. St. Louis saluted his flag with 13 guns. Divisions drilling in Navy Yard. Yard workmen aboard. Liberty and baseball parties ashore. Charleston entered dry-dock at 1.30 p. m.

28th, Tuesday. Partly cloudy and warm. Moored to dock, Navy Yard. Divisions ashore for drill. Commandant of the Navy Yard called on board. Liberty and baseball parties ashore.

29th, Wednesday. Clear and pleasant; warm. Moored to dock, Navy Yard. Commander, Second Division, returned from leave. Commandant of the Navy Yard called officially. Divisions ashore for drill. Yard workmen on board. Liberty and baseball parties ashore.

30th, Thursday. Partly cloudy and pleasant; warm. Moored to dock, Navy Yard. Divisions ashore for drill. Yard workmen on board. Liberty and baseball parties ashore. 2nd and 4th companies returned from American Lake rifle range.

31st, Friday. Fair and pleasant; warm. Moored to dock, Yavy Yard. Baseball and liberty parties ashore. Yard workmen on board. Painting ship.

★ ★ ★

Some egotists this good ship has,
Let's hope we get no more,
For here's the way they sound on board:
i

And here's the way ashore:
I

ITINERARY—U. S. S. TENNESSEE

Port	Arrival	Departure	Miles
League Island, Pa. (com's'd).	July 17, '06	Nov. 1, '06	233
Hampton Roads, Va.	Nov. 3	8	98
Piney Point, Md.	8	8	1834
Colon, Panama.	14	15	130
Chiriqui Lagoon	16	16	1041
Ponce, Porto Rico.	21	22	1285
Hampton Roads, Va.	26	Dec. 16	240
League Island, Pa.	Dec. 18	Apr. 12, '07	233
Hampton Roads, Va.	Apr. 13, '07	14	15
Lynn Haven Bay, Va.	14	16	16
Hampton Roads, Va	16	May 16	530
Provincetown, Mass.	May 18	24	53
Boston, Mass	25	June 5	555
Hampton Roads, Va	June 7	11	382
Newport, R. I.	12	14	3112
Royan, France	23	July 2	52
Ile D' Aix, France	July 2	3	10
La Rochelle, France.	3	11	235
Brest, France	12	25	3194
Tompkinsville, S. I.	Aug. 6	Aug. 16	270

Port	Arrival	Departure	Miles
Hampton Roads, Va.	Aug. 17	Aug. 17	392
Newport, R. I.	18	19	265
Boston, Mass.	20	Sept. 30	265
Newport, R. I.	Oct. 1	Oct. 4	392
Hampton Roads, Va.	5	12	1904
Port of Spain, Trinidad	18	24	3300
Rio de Janeiro, Brazil	Nov. 4	Nov. 10	1044
Montevideo, Uruguay	13	19	1325
Punta Arenas, Chile	23	27	2760
Callao, Peru	Dec. 5	Dec. 12	2240
Acapulco, Mexico	19	22	785
Pichilinque Bay, Mexico	25	28	315
Magdalena Bay, Mexico	29	Feb. 15, '08	1026
San Francisco, Cal	Feb. 20, '08	29	287
Santa Barbara, Cal	Mar. 1	Mar. 6	164
San Diego, Cal	6	16	96
San Pedro, Cal	16	23	18
Redondo, Cal	23	25	9
Venice, Cal	25	27	275
Monterey, Cal	28	29	92
San Francisco, Cal	29	Apr. 1	738
Port Angeles, Wash	Apr. 4	6	36
Port Townsend, Wash	6	8	45
Bellingham, Wash	8	11	32
Blaine, Wash	11	12	87
Everett, Wash	12	13	30
Seattle, Wash	13	17	22
Tacoma, Wash	17	19	26
Puget Sound, Navy Yard	19	May 1	840
San Francisco, Cal	May 4	17	287
Santa Barbara, Cal	18	22	82
San Pedro, Cal	22	25	82
Santa Barbara, Cal	25	28	82
San Pedro, Cal	29	30	28
Venice, Cal	29	June 1	67
Santa Barbara	June 1	5	82
San Pedro	5	12	82
Santa Barbara	13	13	228
Santa Cruz	14	15	91
Carquines Straits	15	25	29
San Francisco	25	July 1	450
San Diego	July 3	7	450
San Francisco	9	12	807
Bremerton	14	....	....

Total, 35,175 Miles

Book Eight

The Volunteer

September 1908

Published Monthly
On Board the
U. S. S. Tennessee

The Flag

OLD Glory waves with love unfurled,
    Her stars and stripes of freedom tell;
She waves in all parts of the world,
    And every nation treats her well.

She proudly waves amid the breeze,
    Scattering friendship everywhere;
And she's known on all the seas,
    For she waves where e'er she cares.

She's first to those when in distress
    And helps where e'er she can;
Teaches right from wickedness—
    For that's the true American.

With a careless wave she seems to know
    That the nation loves her true,
And is with her where e'er she goes,
    To stand by the Red, White and Blue.

—W. S. Gorsuch

Spokane Trophy

CRUISING

August 1st found the Tennessee at the Puget Sound Navy Yard undergoing repairs and preliminary work in connection with the installation of fire control system. The alloted time for repairs at the navy yard expired on August 15th, and all vessels of the First Squadron were under orders to leave for San Francisco about that time.

The Colorado, the first to leave, on the morning of the 15th, met with a serious mishap shortly after passing Seattle. During a thick fog she run aground and was not floated until high water in the afternoon, when it was discovered that it would be necessary to proceed to Puget Sound and be docked for repairs before undertaking the extensive cruise on which she had been ordered.

The Tennessee, Washington and Pennsylvania left at various times on the 16th for San Francisco, for coal and provisions preliminary to joining the Commander-in-Chief for the cruise to Samoa. The vessels did not proceed in squadron, but each made its way down the coast. The weather for the first day was excellent, but about noon of the 17th, a thick fog was encountered, which necessitated proceeding at a slow rate of speed. The fog cleared slightly on the 18th and after speeding up, the Tennessee anchored off California City, in San Francisco Bay, about 8.19 p.m. The West Virginia,

Washington, Pennsylvania and Maryland were at anchor. Coaling gear was rigged that night and on the morning of the 19th, the barque Amy Turner and the schooner Honiper were brought alongside and coaling commenced. The vessels contained narrow hatches and a limited number of whips could be used, so that completion was delayed until Thursday night, 1314 tons having been taken on board. On the 21st, cleaning up occupied the forenoon and at 1 p.m. the ship proceeded to San Francisco, anchoring off the foot of Folsom street. The West Virginia, Maryland, California, South Dakota, Washington, Solace, Buffalo, and the torpedo boat destroyers Whipple, Hull, Truxton, Perry, Preble, Stewart, and Hopkins were at anchor. The ship remained here until the morning of the 24th, when, at 10 a. m., in obedience to signal from the flagship, all ships got underway and stood out of San Francisco harbor. After passing the Golden Gate a thick fog was encountered, which lasted until about 1 p. m., and when abreast the Farallones, each ship, except the Solace stood by to take a torpedo boat in tow for Honolulu. This was accomplished in short order and the ships formed as follows: West Virginia, Flagship of the Commander-in-Chief, with the Preble, Maryland and Perry, Pennsylvania and Stewart, and the Solace; Second Division, Tennessee, Flagship of Division Commander, with the Whipple in tow; Washington and Hopkins, California and Truxton, South Dakota and Hull. About 4 p.m. a stiff breeze set in and held for two days, when, on the 26th, the sea became smooth and the ship finished the balance of the month enroute to Honolulu and the Samoan Islands.

The New Recruit, Two Days Out

<blockquote>
You may have all the ships on the ocean,
No doubt, they are many and grand,
But if they cause people to feel like this,
You can give me a job on the land.
</blockquote>

A ship is called "she" because she is carried away by sales and is only controlled when properly manned.

SEASICKNESS

When the ship puts to sea and the weather gets rough,
When you hide yourself on the gun deck,
When you lie yourself down and you don't care what comes,
When you wish you were hung by the neck,
When your head starts to ache and you feel all cut up,
When you hurry to get on top side,
When you can't guess the trouble and think that perhaps
It may be the effects of the tide—
    YOU'RE SEASICK.

When you wander about and your supper you taste,
Just the same as the time when you ate,
When you make for the rail and the whole thing comes up
At a swift uncontrollable gait,
When your shipmate goes by with a grin on his chops
And tells you of the pork and the string,
It is then that you think of the old country home,
And the officer who swore you in—
    YOU'RE SEASICK.

When you think of a home that was never like this,
When you think of the old village store,
When you dream of the faraway days in '09,
When your cruise in the Navy is o'er,
When you finish a-manning-the-rail, you are weak,
But you'll swear that you're still feeling fine,
You will make double time for the hammock that cures,
Then ship over in 1909—
    YOU'RE SEASICK.

Degree of Completion of Naval Vessels

The degree of completion on August 1st of the vessels under construction for the U. S. Navy was as follows: Battleships, South Carolina, 55; Michigan, 60.4; Delaware, 35.3; North Dakota, 45.7. Scout Cruisers, Salem, 100 (delivered at Navy Yard, Boston, Mass., July 27, 1908). Torpedo boat destroyers, No. 17, 38.7; No. 18, 35.7; No. 19, 42.2; No. 20, .14; No. 21, .14. Submarine torpedo boats, No. 13, 51.9; No. 14, 51.8; No. 15, 50.9; No. 16, 51.1; No. 17, 42.4; No. 18, 41.8; No. 19, 41.3. Colliers, Vestal, 92.8; Prometheus, 71.5. Tugboats, Patapsco, 76; Patuxent, 78.

THE SPOKANE TROPHY

A party of citizens, representing the city of Spokane, Washington, came on board, on August 12th, and, amid appropriate ceremonies, presented the Tennessee with the Spokane Trophy for excellence in turret gunnery, the Tennessee, at the last record practice, having attained the best turret score throughout the entire navy. The cup is a beautiful piece of workmanship and one which we hope will stay with the Tennessee. The Seattle Post-Intelligencer of Aug. 12th contained the following account of the presentation ceremony:

"Mr. D. T. Ham, first vice-president of the Spokane Chamber of Commerce, Mr. Guy D. Groff, of Charles King Camp No. 4, Spanish-American War Veterans, Mr. E. K. Erwin, candidate for the office of State Treasurer, and Mr. L. G. Monroe, Secretary of the Spokane Chamber of Commerce, today presented the cruiser Tennessee with a silver trophy cup given for the highest final record of merit for turret gun marksmanship.

The presentation speech on behalf of the Chamber of Commerce of Spokane was made by Mr. Ham and Mr. G. D. Groff spoke in behalf of the Spanish-American War Veterans. The responses in behalf of the navy were made by Rear Admiral U. Sebree, U. S. Navy, commander of the Second Division, U. S. Pacific Fleet, and Captain Bradley A. Fiske, U. S. Navy, commanding the Tennessee.

The record of the Tennessee was made during the recent target practice in Magdalena Bay. The presentation was made at 2 p. m. The Spokane party was met by an escort of officers and taken aboard ship, where luncheon was served and the ship inspected. Quarters were then sounded and all hands stood at attention during the exercises.

The cup is of solid silver, lined with gold, and stands about two feet high. It is mounted on a rosewood base and on either side of the base is the figure of a gunner stripped to the waist training a miniature 10-inch gun of solid silver, mounted on gold wheels. The bowl is decorated with scenes in and around Spokane and upon one side are figures of President Roosevelt and Secretary of the Navy Metcalf.

The cup will remain in the possession of the Tennessee until the next annual target practice, when it will go to the ship making the highest record for turret gun marksmanship.

The cup was made in Seattle and is considered one of the finest pieces of workmahship of the kind ever turned out in the city."

THE VOLUNTEER

PUBLISHED MONTHLY ABOARD THE U. S. S. TENNESSEE

J. E. ERWIN.........................PUBLISHER

VOL. 1 NO. 8   HONOLULU, H. I., SEPT., 1908   PRICE, 15c

ORIGIN OF THE COMPASS

The early history of the compass is involved in more or less obscurity. In rough form it was known to the Chinese as early as 2634 B. C. and it was used for the purpose of navigation as early as the third or fourth century A. D., and perhaps before. But the policy of the rulers and the habits and character of the people conspired to render the Chinese indifferent navigators, and the compass did not, therefore, become of the great importance to them that it did to the seafaring nations of Europe.

The date of introduction of the magnetic needle is unknown, but if it came, as many suppose, from the Chinese through the Arab sailors and traders, it probably was already a nautical instrument.

The first reference to it in literature is in a work by Alexander Neckam, entitled "De Utensilibus," and written in the twelfth century. He refers to it as a needle which is placed on a pivot and when allowed to come to rest shows the mariner the direction to steer. In another work, "De Naturis Rerum," he writes as follows: "Mariners at sea, when, through cloudy weather in the day, which hides the sun, or through the darkness of the night, they lose the knowledge of the quarter of the world to which they are sailing, touch a needle with a magnet, which will turn around, till, on its motion ceasing, its point will be directed toward the north."

As early as the thirteenth century it seems to have been known to the navigators of all European nations, and in 1269 its declination (or variation from the true north) seems to have been observed.

DAILY LOG FOR AUGUST, 1908

Saturday, August 1. Partly cloudy and fair. Moored to dock, Navy Yard, Puget Sound. Yard workmen on board. Liberty and baseball parties ashore.

Sunday, August 2. Partly cloudy and hazy. Mustered at usual Sunday quarters and inspection. Served out prize money for excellence in gunnery at last record practice; also, Navy E's for those entitled to wear them. Liberty, baseball, sailing and visiting parties on board. Ship open to visitors; large number on board.

Monday, August 3. Clear and pleasant. Moored to dock, Navy Yard. Yard workmen on board. Baseball and liberty party ashore. Commander H. S. Knapp, commanding the Charleston, called officially.

Tuesday, August 4. Partly cloudy and hazy. Moored to dock at Navy Yard. Yard workmen on board. Had infantry and artillery drill on dock. Commanding Officer of the Charleston called. Liberty, baseball and visiting parties ashore.

Wednesday, August 5. Partly cloudy, warm and pleasant. Moored to dock at Navy Yard. Yard workmen on board. Commander, Second Division, and Commanding Officer called officially on the Charleston. Baseball and liberty parties ashore. Pay-day. Charleston left dock and anchored.

Thursday, August 6th. Partly cloudy and warm. Moored to dock at Navy Yard. Yard workmen on board. Rear Admiral J. K. Barton, U. S. Navy, Chief of Bureau of Steam Engineering, Navy Department, and Captain of Puget Sound Navy Yard, called on board. Navy Yard saluted Rear Admiral Barton with 13 guns. Liberty and baseball parties.

Friday, August 7. Clear, warm and hazy. Moored to dock at Navy Yard. Yard workmen on board. Liberty party ashore.

Saturday, August 8. Fair and warm. Moored to dock at navy yard. Sent party to attend annual clam bake given at Tacoma, Wash., by the crew of the Washington. Yard workmen on board.

Sunday, August 9. Clear and pleasant. Moored to dock at Navy Yard. Mustered at Sunday quarters for inspection. Chaplain held divine service. Liberty party ashore. Ship opened to visitors; many on board.

Monday, August 10. Partly cloudy and hazy. Moored to dock at navy yard. Wheeling and Princeton were brought in and moored to dock. Yard workmen on board. Liberty party ashore.

Tuesday, August 11. Partly cloudy and hazy to overcast. Moored to dock at navy yard. Yard workmen on board. Liberty party ashore.

Wednesday, August 12. Overcast; cloudy and rainy. Moored to dock at navy yard. Rear Admiral W. L. Capps, U. S. Navy, Chief of Bureau of Construction and Repair, called on board. Received delegation of citizens from Spokane, Wash., who presented the ship with the Spokane trophy for excellence in turret marksmanship. Yard workmen on board. Received two lighters of coal alongside.

Thursday, August 13. Overcast and cloudy. Moored to dock at navy yard. Coaling ship; took on board 400 tons. Cleaning up after coaling. Yard workmen on board. Liberty party ashore.

Friday, August 14. Fair and pleasant. Moored to dock at navy yard. Yard workmen on board. Liberty and baseball parties ashore.

Saturday, August 15. Clear and pleasant. Moored to dock at navy yard and at anchor off navy yard. Colorado got underway at 6 a. m. and left harbor. Yard workmen on board. Baseball and liberty party ashore. Left dock at 5.10 p. m. and anchored off navy yard. Pennsylvania and Washington left dock and anchored in stream.

Sunday, August 16. Partly cloudy and fair to clear, cool and pleasant. At anchor off navy yard, Puget Sound, and underway for San Francisco. At 6.30 a. m. the Oregon was brought in and moored to dock. Charleston got underway and moored to dock at 7 a. m. Got underway at 8.11 a. m. and left harbor. Anchored at 9.02 on account of thick fog. Discovered stowaway on board and sent him ashore in shore boat. Got underway at 9.30 and stood out. Rounded Cape

Flattery at 5.18 p. m. Washington in sight.

Monday, August 17. Cloudy, foggy, overcast and damp. At sea, enroute for San Francisco, Cal. At 1 p. m. ran into thick fog. Slowed down on account of fog. Sounding fog whistle throughout day.

Tuesday, August 18. Foggy to overcast and cloudy last part. At sea, enroute for San Francisco and at anchor off California City, Cal. At 10 a. m. fog cleared a little and went ahead at increased speed. Sighted steamer and tow bound north; also numerous sailing vessels. Sighted Farrallones at 5.25 p. m., entered San Francisco bay and anchored off California City, Cal., at 8.19 p. m. West Virginia, Maryland, Pennsylvania and Washington at anchor. Rigged coaling gear.

Wednesday, August 19. At anchor, California City, Cal. Cloudy and overcast to clear and pleasant. At 8 a. m. saluted the Commander-in-Chief, Pacific Fleet, with 13 guns; returned by West Virginia. Solace passed up for San Francisco; Hull and Truxton passed down for Mare Island. Division Commander and Commanding Officer called on the Commander-in-Chief. West Virginia and Maryland left for San Francisco. Coaling ship from schooner Honiper and barque Amy Turner.

Thursday, August 20. Overcast and cloudy to clear and pleasant. Washington left for San Francisco. Coaling ship. Received draft from Independence and transferred short-time men to the Independence. Assistant Paymaster E. A. Cobey, U. S. N., reported on board. Baseball team ashore. Finished coaling; took 1314 tons on board.

Friday, August 21. Partly cloudy and cool. At anchor off California City, underway for and at anchor off San Francisco. Cleaning ship after coaling. Received draft of marines from Mare Island. Got underway at 1 p. m. and anchored in fleet formation off San Francisco at 2.06 p.m. Chief of Staff and Commanding Officer of Maryland called on board. Buffalo came in, anchored and saluted with 13 guns, returned by West Virginia. Pennsylvania came in and anchored.

Saturday, August 22. Overcast and hazy to partly cloudy and pleasant. At anchor off San Francisco, Cal. Received draft of men from Constellation. Division Commander called on Maryland. Stewart came in and anchored. Buffalo left harbor.

Sunday, August 23. Fair and cool to overcast and cloudy. At anchor off San Francisco. Commanding Officer called on West Virginia, Maryland, California and South Dakota. Received draft of men from Pensacola. Mustered at quarters and had inspection. Chaplain held divine service.

Monday, August 24. At anchor off San Francisco and enroute for Honolulu. Partly cloudy and pleasant to foggy, then clear and cool. Stiff breeze last part. All ships got underway at 10.05 a.m. except Whipple and left harbor. At 12.45 formed line of divisions. Thick fog encountered off San Francisco Lightship. At 1.30 ran out of fog and took torpedo boat destroyers in tow, Whipple having joined in meantime. Went ahead, each ship towing destroyer, except Solace; formation line of divisions, 3000 yards, 1000 yards interval. Breeze increased to moderate gale during last part.

Tuesday, August 25. Partly cloudy, stiff breeze. At sea, enroute to Honolulu. Steaming in same formation, with torpedo boat destroyers in tow.

Wednesday, August 26. Clear and pleasant. Enroute to Honolulu. Changed uniform for crew from blue to white undress. In formation throughout day towing the Whipple. Pacific Mail Steamer Manchuria passed about 6.30 p.m. bound for Honolulu.

Thursday, August 27. Clear and pleasant. Smooth sea. At sea, enroute to Honolulu. At 5 a.m. West Virginia lost man overboard; was recovered. Same formation.

Friday, August 28. Fair and pleasant. At sea, enroute to Honolulu. Clear and pleasant. Smooth sea. Steaming in same formation.

Saturday, August 29. Partly cloudy and pleasant. At sea, enroute to Honolulu. Ships stopped to send fresh provisions to destroyers. Steamer Alameda passed, bound to San Francisco. Steaming in same formation. Passed sailing ship.

Sunday, August 30. Partly cloudy to overcast and rainy. At sea, enroute to Honolulu. Mustered at Sunday quarters and had inspection. Chaplain held divine service. Steaming in same formation with tows. Passed steamer bound north.

Monday, August 31. Partly cloudy and pleasant. At sea, enroute to Honolulu. Steaming in same formation. Distance to go to Honolulu from noon, 482 miles.

OUR FIRST WAR VESSELS

The outbreak of the Revolutionary war found the patriots without a navy. Congress tried to create one. Four merchantmen were first purchased, equipped with guns, and sent to sea as cruisers, but their defects as war vessels soon became so apparent that Congress determined at once to set about the building of a navy. On October 3, 1775, Congress ordered two cruisers built, and on December 13th the order was increased to five thirty-two gun ships, five twenty-eight gun ships and three twenty-four gun ships. They were to be ready for the sea by the following April. The names given to the thirteen vessels were Boston, Congress, Effingham, Delaware, Hancock, Montgomery, Providence, Raleigh, Trumbull, Virginia, Warren, Washington and Randolph. These were the first war vessels constructed in the United States. The first commander-in-chief was Ezekiel Hopkins, of Rhode Island, a young brother of Congressman Stephen Hopkins. He was appointed to this high office on December 22, 1775.

GUNPOWDER

The explosion of gunpowder is divided into three distinct stages, called the ignition, inflammation and combustion. The ignition is the setting on fire of the first grain, while the inflammation is the spreading of the flame over the surface of the powder from the point of ignition; combustion is the burning up of each grain. The value of gunpowder is due to the fact that when subjected to sufficient heat it becomes a gas which expands with frightful rapidity. The so called explosion that takes place when a match is touched to gunpowder is merely a chemical change during which there is a sudden evolution of gases from the original solid. It has been calculated that ordinary gunpowder on exploding expands about 9,000 times, or fills a space this much larger as a gas than when in a solid form. When this chemical change takes place in a closed vessel, this expansion may be made to do a work like that of forcing a projectile along the bore of the great gun in the lines of the least resistance.

THE BASEBALL WORLD

The excitement in the contest for the championship of the Second Division of the Pacific Fleet still continues to be at a high pitch, and at the time of going to press the winner has not been decided.

The following games, which count in the series, have been played during the month:

At Puget Sound Navy Yard.—Aug. 1: Tennessee 2, Washington 1; Aug. 5: Tennessee 3, Washington 5.

At San Francisco, Cal.—Aug. 22: Tennessee 7, South Dakota 1.

The games between the Tennessee and Washington were hotly contested and great rivalry existed. Each ship sent its band and every available rooter to bring back victory. In the last game of the series, which, if won by the Tennessee would have put the Washington behind the California by one game, was one of the best games of baseball seen on the Bremerton grounds in many days.

In the seventh inning, with two men out and two strikes on the batter, Blahos was touched up for a two-base hit which scored two of the Washington's men, and several more hits resulted in five runs for the Washington to one for the Tennessee. In the eighth the Tennessee made another spurt and put over two runs, but the lead of the Washington could not be wiped out and that team won.

STANDING OF SECOND DIVISION TEAMS.

Washington	10	7	3	.700
California	10	6	4	.600
Tennessee	7	4	3	.571
South Dakota	7	0	7	.000

The Washington defeated the California on the 21st of August by a score of 5 to 3, which puts the California out of the contest. By defeating the South Dakota in the two remaining games it will be necessary for the Washington to again defeat the Tennessee before she is entitled to the division championship. This game should prove a good one and here is luck to the Tennessee.

CHANGES FOR AUGUST, 1908

Received on Board

Amos, Otto L, os
Audibert, E P, cp
Bowen, W, cp
Brady, P G, f2c
Boesch, M J, os
Barnes, E, os
Bishupski, F C, os
Brooks, D R, cp
Brayman, S L, cp
Beck, J W, cp
Brady, L, cp
Braun, H A, cp
Barry, W B, cp
Bowen, W F, cp
Beech, W A, cp
Carey, A H, os
Conyers, D E, os
Czar, E, os
Cwalino, J, cp
Coughlin, J J, cp
Colbath, J A, cp
Colbath, A C, cp
Desmond, W E, os
Donohue, J J, os
Daubert, A E, cp
Dunham, R, cp
Eddins, H M, mm2c
Fitzpatrick, H, f2c
Farraday, W, os
Furman, J W, os
Faith, R, os
Grant, E H, os
Gilson, T, cp
Garland, J B, cp
Grant, E H, cp
Goerke, E, ctc
Gavette, G A, cp
Hayes, A, wt
Hoencke, T H, swrt
Holcombe, C W, os
Hickey, J M, os
Harper, J M, cp
Hawley, H L, cp
Heany, J F, cp
Hobson, R R, cp
Howard, J H, cp
Hennessy, F, os
Ironside, F E, cp
Long, H, cp
Lafrenaye, J E, cp
Myers, M E, cp
Michelsen, E J, os
Moore, A R, cp
Mitchell, W H, cp
Merrill, H M, cp
McDonald, J C, os
McFarlane, G, cp
McFetridge, F D, cp
McDonald, J T, cp
Nelson, L A, mus2c
Noll, C A, os
O'Connell, J J, cp
Perreault, C G C, os
Powers, B M, cp
Riley, C, os
Rainville, J O, os
Reichenback, W H, cp
Rich, J E, os
Riley, L, os
Stein, S, f1c
Solomon, J W, matt3c
Shunk, S, os
Smith, C, os
Schroth, J, cp
Spring, H J, cp
Swope, L A, cp
Schmidt, F, cp
Shirley, C J, cp
Sullivan, J, bm1c
Sewell, W S, os
Schad, P, os
Scheu, J H, os
Stuby, C F, os
Spedding, J W, os
Trabert, G, bmkr
Timmins, W M, cp

Thomas, J J, os
Thatcher, T W, gm1c
Underhill, E G, cp
Uhrig, F L, os
Varley, T H, os
Vermillyae, R E, cp
Van Vleet, W, os
Whitaker, C R, swrt
Wilson, F H, el3c
Watson, L, cmm
Wurdig, E, os

Weir, D, os
Wilson, H E, os
Wright, G W, os
Weaver, G C, cp
Weiss, J J, cp
Weishan, C, os
Walsh, R D, os
Williams, J R, os
Wathen, G T, os
Zimmerman, W C, os

Transferred

Schmidt, F C, gm3c
    Nav Hos, Bremerton
Byram, T P, yeo2c
    Philadelphia
Dodge, R A, os
    Franklin
Madison, J V, bm2c
    Wabash
Bevan, C, el3c
    Washington
Wilson, F H, el3c
    Washington
Cook, J D, el3c
    South Dakota

To the Independece:
  Kohlman, H W C, swrt
  Austin, G, cgm
  O'Sullivan, M, pvt
  Smith, S B, pvt
  Daily, W J, oil
  Cunti, F, music
  Breslen, G, cox
  Wolf, L, wt
  Rasmussen, G, oil
  Rosthchild, L S, cmm
  Neilson, A, f1c

Discharged

Stevens, H E, os
Borg, A E, qm1c
Ebersberger, A J N, os

O'Brien, P, wt
Hill, J T, bak2c
Neilson, J, os

Changes in Rating

Byram, T P, yeo 3c to 2c
Taylor, V H, sea to qm3c
McCabe, W E, sea to cox
Pauly, N J, sea to cox
Stein, M L, cox to sea
Schmidt L, bak 2c to 1c
Maine, F H, os to bak 2c
Reinhold, W, f1c to wt
Teubert, C J, f2c to f1c
Dwyer, J J "
Valicenti, N "
Deaver, W O "
Stone, J J G "
Birx, F "

Clark, E W, f2c to f1c
McDonald, J J "
Young, J A "
Matthies, J "
Ricks, P "
Wallace, J A "
Thomas, S H "
White, W H "
Upsher, J P "
McClure, F W "
Wing, F R "
Weiss, L P "
Knickerbocker, L S

Changes in Rating -- Continued

Naugle, C B,	cp to f2c	Showalter, N P,	cp to f2c
Stoner, S	"	Brauer, F C	"
Kurtz, H C	"	Rasch, F W	"
Mayhue, W E	"	Mays, W	"
Simpson, W W	"	Whitaker, H	"
Gable, W C	"	Hamilton, F	"
Gentel, J A	"	Chanelli, N	"
Myrick, A E	"	Jones, J T	"
Blaknee, F	"	Laverty, S H	"
Matture, W M	"	Woltz, C O	"
Ryan, M W	"	Wagner, P	"
Searle, G W	"	Malinowski, J	"
Gorsuch, W S	"	Gibbs, J J	"
Maurer, J B	"	Smith, G M	"
Wilson, H A	"	Myers, J. S.	"
Kelly, H	"	Halley, J J	"
Morris, J McC	"	McCullough, S A	"
Barry, D F	"	Carter, F	"
Lawler, C T	"	Koehler, J E	"
Charlton, T S	"	Norman, C D	"
Wasserman, F C	"	Williams, M E	"
Aufiero, P	"	Fachting, L W	"
Butler, G	"	Bunch, H	"
Henry, H F	"	Schroeder, P C	"
Jones, W M	"	Matture, F	"
Kummerow, J	"	Carnahan, W E	"
Beattie, T B	"	Moeller, A W,	os to el3c
Ferciger, J	"	Volz, H L,	cp to el3c
Miller, J J	"	Prestwood, J G,	sea to el3c
Lotz, H L	"		

IN 1812.

Jack Tar was a toper,
A regular old doper,
Sez he to himself with a smack,
I often times snicker
When out of red liquor,
But I hates to be out on shellac.

To the Newcomers: 3-10 and a butt. Cheer up, boys, we all started there.

In Samoa.—Well, did you draw your blade and run him through. Liberty man, after springing a whopper: I did, all but the last two words, believe me.

THE MID-WATCH.

He sat upon the galley hatch,
His eyes were growing dim,
The boatswain's mate yelled "ash-whip,"
And then made a pass at him.

Five p. m. of the first day out. Oh no! I'm not seasick, only I do not want any supper.

The Tennessee's sport in the Frisco restaurant: Waiter, the proprietor should learn to spell, he has written omelette with one tea instead of two. All right, said the waiter, I'll take it back. He returned in a few minutes: "Omelet" 50 cents, 2 teas, 40 cents.

When your shipmate says "I am so short,"
And starts the same old song,
Don't wait to hear how short he is
But just reply "So long."

The Engineer's force having purchased a phonograph, it is becoming customary for the sentimental chaps to buy a late record when on shore. Recently in San Francisco, one of the men wandered into a grocery store, by mistake, and called for a record. The proprietor, somewhat astonished, directed him to a music store. The fireman, not wishing to be joshed, said "I understood preserved tongue was kept in grocery stores."

ITINERARY, U. S. PACIFIC FLEET

August 24th to December 4th, 1908.

Leave	San Francisco, Cal.	Aug. 24	
Arrive	Honolulu, H. I.	Sept. 2	2100
Leave	" "	" 10	
Arrive	Pago Pago	" 20	2263
Leave	" "	" 27	
Arrive	Honolulu, H. I.	Oct. 7	2263
Leave	" "	" 17	
Arrive	San Diego, Cal.	" 28	2280
Leave	" "	" 30	
Arrive	Magdalena Bay, Mex.	Nov. 1	585
Leave	" " "	" 30	
Arrive	San Francisco, Cal.	Dec. 4	1012

Total No. Miles, 10,503

NOTES.

While at Pago Pago, two armored cruisers and two destroyers will visit Apia for two days. The four vessels to make this visit will be designated by the Commander-in-Chief upon arrival at Pago Pago.

Dates of departure are fixed; dates of arrival may vary according to ease or difficulty with which destroyers are towed.

VESSELS TO GO.

First Division—West Virginia, Maryland and Pennsylvania. Second Division—Tennessee, Washington, California and South Dakota. First Torpedo Flotilla—Truxton, Hull, Whipple and Hopkins. Second Torpedo Flotilla—Perry, Preble and Stewart. Torpedo Supply Ship—Solace. Colliers—Saturn and Justin, to Honolulu only.

Distance traveled to August 1, 35,175 miles.

ITINERARY FOR AUGUST

Navy Yard, Puget Sound		Aug. 16	840
California City, Cal.	Aug. 18	Aug. 21	9
San Francisco, Cal.	Aug. 21	Aug. 24	

Book Nine

The November 1908 Volunteer

Magdalena Bay, Mexico

 Published Monthly On Board the U. S. S. Tennessee

The
Flagship Tennessee

Where music thrills our souls tonight,
  Where hearts are beating free,
We'll pledge the navy's shining light—
  The Flagship Tennessee!

Let every glass be filled abrim,
  Let every one decree
His fealty to our cruiser trim—
  The Flagship Tennessee!

The Chief of that division strong
  Is Admiral Sebree;
May he that honor wield for long
  On board the Tennessee!

The man of nerve to take a risk,
  Whate'er the chance may be,
Is Captain Bradley Allen Fiske—
  Who guides the Tennessee!

May officers and men live long,
  In this may they agree—
To love and praise with fervor strong
  The Flagship Tennessee!

With every glassfull sparkling bright,
  Let's drink in love and glee
To our fair queen afloat tonight—
  The Flagship Tennessee!

             Sincerely,
         (Signed) C. P. Rees.

Honolulu, T. H.,
  October 21st, 1908.

The Volunteer

 ## Cruising

IN 1889 a treaty was formed which gave equal rights to British, Americans and Germans, acknowledged the Samoan independence, and established a court of justice. Apia was made capital. King Malietoa returned in 1889 and was again made king, remaining until his death, Aug. 22, 1898. In 1899 a dispute arose in electing a successor to the deceased king and the three interested nations formed a treaty which bears the date of Dec. 2nd, giving the United States the Island of Tutuila and all land in the Samoan group east of the 171st parallel. Germany obtained the Island of Upolu and Savii and all land in the Samoans west of the 171st parallel. The British relinquished their rights in Samoa to the Germans for which they obtained Germany's interests in the Solomon Group and territory about the Volta river in Africa, but reserved a coaling station and other rights until the Boer war when they gave up all rights to Germany and the United States.

Germany governs the Islands of Savii and Upolu and adjacent islets by a territorial governor and a native chief and consul. The Islands of Tutuila and the Mauna Group and islets are governed by the United States, which power is vested in a Naval Governor. The population consists of about 40,000—Upolu has 16,600, Savaii, 14,000, and Tutuila and Mauna, 4,500. Of the whites there are about 200 British, 300 Germans, 100 Americans and 25 French. The remainder of the population consists of natives and Polynesians.

Cotton, sugar, coffee and cocoanuts are the principal exports; also, copra, made from the cocoanut, and used in the manufacture of cocoanut oil.

Apia, Capital of German Samoa, is a very inviting place looking in from the sea. The harbor is not an excellent one; it is formed by coral reef with a narrow entrance. Little protection is afforded for large vessels. The city lies in a long crescent like shape along a ridge close to the beach. The houses near the water are mostly white and are surrounded by palms and flowers.

The flags from the many consulates are seen flying and all things considered it is a pretty little city until one visits it. There is but one street from Matautu to Mulinuu and along this live the Europeans and are also the places of administration. On the left are the American Consulate and English Mission Church. On the left are the German Consulate buildings and in the center is the Roman Catholic Mission Church, made from blocks of white coral taken from the reef. This is an important landmark for ships making the harbor. About one-half mile distant from the church in the rear is a college where boys are educated for the missionary. Back of the street is the native village.

The natives were interested in the large ships and gazed with wonder on the many different devices. They appear to be a kind race and have a decided desire for knowledge in all lines.

Liberty was granted to 150 men from each cruiser and to the destroyer crews. The little city outdid many of the larger ones in the way of entertainment, the following program having been arranged and nicely carried out:

Sept. 21st. 2 p.m.—Public Talolo and Samoan dances in Mulinuu. 8.30 p.m.—Bierabend at Tivoli hotel for officers.

Sept. 22nd. 9 a.m.—Races at Matafagatele. 2 p.m.—(Taumafataga) Samoan feast in Apia village. 8 p.m.—Ball for officers at Central hotel.

As the natives were interested in the ships, so the crew was interested in the natives, and with wonder nearly all gazed on the native dances and customs. Many of them came aboard the ship with native products for sale and seemed to enjoy immensely the change of life from the dull Samoan routine to the activity of a modern cruiser.

While the stay in Apia lasted but two days, it was thoroughly enjoyable, and, almost to a man, we regretted, on the morning of the 23rd, to depart for Pago Pago, Tutuila.

Pago Pago is a beautiful little harbor, located in Tutuila, the largest of the U. S. possessions in Samoa, and it is really the only excellent harbor in the entire group, being entirely land locked and protected on all sides by the almost perpendicular hills which extend skyward to a distance of from two thousand to three thousand feet. On the point, overlooking the entrance, is the Governor's house, and farther in on the left, are the well kept grounds and trim spar colored buildings of the Naval Station. The natives in the several villages located on the shores of the harbor flocked to the Tennessee, as the great ship moored to the Naval Station dock, the Washington having anchored off the Governor's house, and the destroyers Whipple and Hopkins proceeding to the torpedo boat anchorage in the upper end of the harbor. Here, in the little harbor of Pago Pago, protected on all sides, rested the strength of the great Pacific Fleet.

Pago Pago harbor is of marvelous depth, and the harbor seems to have been formed, and it is so claimed by many, from the crater or craters of extinct volcanoes. If this is true, nature has here performed one of her most wonderful works.

On Sept. 24th, at 10 a.m., the natives gave a Fono, followed at 2 p.m. by a feast and Siva, as a welcome to the officers of the fleet. This was followed, on Friday, by a Talolo, or gift festival, followed by a siva; the entertainment afforded being odd and decidedly enjoyable. A large number of the natives had come from surrounding villages in war canoes, some on the station ship Annapolis, and others had walked to take part in the welcome.

That the Samoans are a poetic people can hardly be disputed, as is evidenced by the almost perfect chant which they sing without the aid of music of any kind. As the many war canoes circled the ships singing in the low chant of the natives, the sound was strikingly peculiar, and while many smiled, the native Samoan, from deep down in his soul, was telling of the mighty power, beauty and achievements of the great Amerika, and bidding all a welcome to Samoa.

The dances given by the natives were close enough to the ship to be witnessed by all, and it was a rare treat to one who had never witnessed a similar event.

Liberty was granted to 60 men from each vessel daily, and many of the boys took advantage of an opportunity to see the beautiful island, wandering from village to village, gazing with wonder on the land that they had read of in books, very few men of the entire fleet ever having visised Samoa prior to this time. Here indeed was a curiosity for the liberty party, a place where money could not be spent, differing widely from the many ports visited where the other extreme is almost always in evidence. The natives were allowed on board each day and they came in droves; more to the Tennessee than other vessels perhaps, as it did not require much exertion to get on board from the dock. The native seemed indeed to be a peculiar being, almost devoid of clothing, except for the lava lava (a cloth girdling the hips), and each with his bundle of native wares, consisting mainly of tapa cloth, kavir bowls, mats, war clubs, beads and shells, ever willing to sell or barter for money or something from Amerika. The value of money, judging from our native visitors, is hardly appreciated by the Samoan, since articles with money values of from £2 to £4 were readily exchanged for an old coat with shiny buttons, and war clubs, valued at 4 and 6 shillings, were exchanged for "one soap or tobac."

At the Naval Station there is a native guard, called the Fita Fita, enlisted in the service of Uncle Sam, and they perform the guard duty about the station, as well as augment the crew of the station ship Annapolis while on trips to the neighboring islands. They are a well drilled body of men and represent the flower of the island.

The Fleet had been scheduled to remain here but seven days, from September 20th to 27th, but colliers chartered to bring coal from Hampton Roads had encountered heavy weather, the Strathyre arriving on September 26th and the Strathleven on October 3rd. The West Virginia and tow, followed by the Maryland, Pennsylvania and South Dakota, coaled from the Strathyre and on October 3rd sailed for Honolulu. The remaining vessels commenced coaling from the Strathleven on the 3rd and on the 7th sailed for Honolulu, leaving the great harbor of Pago Pago to shelter the little station ship Annapolis.

The Solace having left the formation to proceed to Suva in order to cable the arrival of the squadron at Pago Pago, picked up the fleet by wireless on September 25th, and reported that the British S.S. Aeon, having Chaplain Patrick, his wife and family, and Mrs. W. K. Riddle, wife of Lieutenant Riddle, of the Tutuila Naval Station, on board, had been wrecked on Christmas Island on July 18, 1908, and were then enroute to Suva on the British S.S. Manuka. Christmas Island is an unhabited island, but enough food, water and wreckage was saved from the Aeon to enable the party to live comfortably until the officers of the Aeon made Fanning Island, a distance of 165 miles, in an open boat, and were there enabled to communicate by wireless with the Manuka to go to the rescue and with Suva, Fijii Islands, by cable. The Solace entered the harbor on the 26th and, after discharging provisions to the fleet, sailed on the 27th for Suva, to bring the shipwrecked party to Tutuila. As the remainder of the fleet cleared the harbor on October 7th, communication was established with the Solace enroute to Pago Pago with the party on board and all well.

The cruise to Honolulu was uneventful, the Tennessee, Washington and California taking their tows and steaming along at about 10 knots, until the 14th, when the destroyers cast off and proceeded under their own steam. The ships were in communication with the Solace and with the West Virginia during the entire voyage. On the 15th, heavy weather was encountered, and the Hopkins was taken in tow by the Washington, the California proceeding, in company with the Whipple and Truxtun to Honolulu, where they arrived early on the 17th, the Tennessee, Washington and Hopkins arriving about noon. The Tennessee immediately entered the harbor and moored to the Oceanic wharf.

The stay in Honolulu, though short, was exceedingly pleasant. A ball to the enlisted men of the fleet was given on the 20th, at the Seaside Hotel, and it was voted a very good time. One of the features was the music furnished by the combined bands of the Second Division ships and applause was always in order. A ball was given by the ladies of Honolulu to the chief petty officers of the fleet. This event occurred on the roof garden of the Alexander Young Hotel, and was very enjoyable, a great many of the chief petty officers attending. Athletic events, which are more fully described on other pages, were arranged and carried off successfully.

All the ships having been coaled and provisioned, the order to get underway was given on the morning of the 22nd, and the cruisers, augmented by the Colorado, picked up their tows, for the last leg of the long journey, and straightened out in cruising formation on the course for Magdalena Bay, orders having been received that cancelled the trip to San Diego, Cal. The Solace remained at Honolulu for mail to rejoin the fleet at sea.

On November 1st the squadron was in latitude 25°-02′, longitude 115°-39′, distant 182 miles from Magdalena Bay, whither they were bound for target practice.

THE NOVEMBER VOLUNTEER

Description of Cuts

The following half-tone cuts are used in the make-up of this issue:—

Page 2.—Pacific Fleet at anchor in Pago Pago harbor. Tennessee can be seen tied up to the Naval Station dock at extreme right.

Page 8.—Governor's House, Pago Pago, on knoll at left.

Page 13.—Showing construction of a Samoan house.

Page 15.—Samoan chief and his wife.

While going on the bridge last night,
I got an awful sudden fright
Said Wrightson, with a frown.
You know as I was climbing there;
The thing I saw that caused my scare,
Was the bridge clock running down.

An automobile and 25 cts. for supper. Never mind, Henry, the Fifth division knows you're a sport.

Right face, said the Sergeant to the Rookie Marine. The Rook: This is all the one I have, sir.

Oysters come high in Honolulu, Rudolph, but you had to have them, and besides you looked right nice sitting in the Alexander Young Hotel. You're from Pittsburg, I'll bet ten cents.

Note.—The red ink on the cover of this month's "Volunteer" came from—well, just ask any of the Fifth division painters (?).

THE VOLUNTEER

PUBLISHED MONTHLY ABOARD THE U. S. S. TENNESSEE

J. E. ERWIN .... PUBLISHER

Vol. 1 No. 10 { MAGDALENA BAY, MEX., NOVEMBER, 1908 } PRICE, 15c

Save Your Money

Save your money, boys! One of the essential points in a cruise in our Navy is to go out so that we may be independent until we obtain employment or re-enlist. Soon some of us will be going home again and we want to go appearing like a representative of a great institution, and with a pocket full of money. We may re-enlist again, many of us will, yet there is every reason why we should, during the time we are home, endeavor to reflect credit on our service. Some of us will not come back again, but our savings will tide us over until we can obtain a good position in civil life, or may be help us engage in some business. There are lots of opportunities in civil life for the hustling young man, even without money, but there are more for the man with a few dollars, and we must, if we desire to be good citizens, be able to seize one of these opportunities.

Interest on a few dollars for a few years will work wonders to make one independent. If you have not started a bank account, why not do so now? Either make an allotment or place a portion of your monthly pay in the ship's bank at 4 per cent. Have you ever experienced the important feeling of a man with a bank account; better try it—may be you will be surprised.

Two years on an enlistment will soon pass, even though it may seem a long time, and, unless we have made preparations for the day we are discharged, we must either hustle for employment or rethrn again before our well earned vacation has been enjoyed.

A small bank account is an excellent thing to have, and if you have not started, think it over and begin at once.

Daily Log

Thursday, September 24. Overcast, cloudy and rainy. Moored to dock, Pago Pago, Tutuila, Samoa. Held mine practice. Large number of natives on board.

Friday, 25th. Partly cloudy and warm with passing showers. Moored to dock, Pago Pago. S.S. Dawn from Apia, came in at 7 a. m. Governor of Tutuila called officially and was saluted with 17 guns. District Governors called on Division Commander. At 2 p.m. Commander, Second Division, Captain and officers went ashore to attend native Talalo. Mining party and diving party out. Large number of natives on board. Liberty party ashore.

Saturday, 26th. Overcast and warm, passing showers. General field day. At 10 a.m. British S.S. Strathyre, with coal for fleet, came in and went alongside West Virginia; commenced coaling that vessel. Preble went alongside Strathyre and commenced coaling. Solace came in from Suva. Sent party to Solace for stores and fresh beef. Liberty party ashore. Natives on board. At 5.45 p.m. S.S. Dawn sailed.

Sunday, 27th. Cloudy and warm with light breezes; occasional showers. Moored to dock, Pago Pago. Commander-in-Chief, U. S. Pacific Fleet, called officially. Mustered at Sunday quarters for inspection. Chaplain held divine service. Received stores from Solace. West Virginia finished coaling and collier went alongside Maryland at 4.15 p.m. Stewart went alongside collier.

Monday, 28th. Overcast and heavy rain. Moored to dock, Pago Pago. Sent diving party out. Marines went ashore for battalion drill. Stewart left collier. Quarters at 1.15 p.m. served out hammocks. Midshipmen D. S. H. Howard and S. B. McKinney went to Pennsylvania for temporary duty.

Tuesday, 29th. Overcast and warm with rain. Moored to dock, Pago Pago. Maryland finished coaling and collier went to Pennsylvania. Whipple went alongside collier. South Dakota and Maryland got underway and changed berths. Commander-in-Chief and Division Commander called officially on Governor of Eastern Division of the Island.

Wednesday, 30th. Partly cloudy and warm, with occasional showers. Moored to dock, Pago Pago. At 6 a.m. S.S. Dawn came in from Apia. Hopkins got underway, shifted berth and broke quarantine flag. Whipple left collier and Hull went alongside at 10 a.m. Baseball and liberty parties ashore. Natives on board. Had searchlight exercise from 8 to 8.30 p.m.

Thursday, 1. Cloudy and warm, showers last part. Moored to dock, Pago Pago, Samoa. Whipple, Hull and South Dakota coaling from collier Strathyre. Liberty party ashore. Natives aboard.

Friday, 2. Partly cloudy and pleasant, with showers. Moored to dock, Pago Pago. Board of Examiners for Gunners met. South Dakota finished coaling. Strathyre shoved off and anchored. Liberty party ashore. Large number of natives on board.

Saturday, 3. Partly cloudy and warm, with passing showers. Moored to dock, Pago Pago. General field day. British S.S. Strathleven, with coal for fleet, came in at 10 a.m., and went alongside California and commenced coaling that vessel. Visiting parties sent to Pennsylvania and South Dakota. Liberty party ashore. Large number of natives on board.

Sunday, 4. Fair and warm. Moored to dock, Pago Pago. West Virginia, Pennsylvania, Maryland, South Dakota, with their respective tows, Preble, Perry, Stewart and Hull, got underway at 10 a.m. and sailed for Honolulu. Mustered at Sunday quarters for inspection. Chaplain held divine service. At 1.30 p.m. Washington shifted to berth vacated by South Dakota. California finished coaling. Strathleven left California and went alongside Washington to coal that vessel. Truxtun went alongside collier to coal. Liberty party ashore. Large number of natives aboard.

Monday, 5. Partly cloudy and warm. Moored to dock, Pago Pago. Rigged coaling gear. Washington and Truxtun finished coaling. Strathleven left Washington and came alongside. Commenced coaling at 6.30 p.m. and stopped at 9 p.m. Took 285 tons.

Tuesday, 6. Overcast, cool and rainy. Moored to dock, Pago Pago. Commenced coaling at 5.30 a.m., finished at 9 p.m.; took 1500 tons.

Wednesday, 7. Partly cloudy and warm, with frequent showers. Moored to dock, Pago Pago, and at sea, enroute to Honolulu, T. H. Rigged in boats in morning watch and prepared for sea. General field day. At 9.31 a.m. cast off lines from dock and stood out with Washington and California, inverted order, 500 yards, torpedo boat destroyers Whipple, Hopkins and Truxtun 500 yards on starboard hand of parent ship. At 12.43 signalled division to pick up tows. Whipple fast at 1.04 p.m. Went ahead standard speed 10½ knots, for Honolulu. At 10 p.m. California lost tow.

Thursday, 8. Partly cloudy and warm. At sea, enroute to Honolulu. On course towing Whipple, in line, distance 2000 yards. California picked up tow at daylight and regained position. Had collision drill.

No. 98 Building a Samoan house.

Friday, 9. Partly cloudy and pleasant. At sea, enroute to Honolulu. In line towing Whipple. Had sub-caliber practice and collision drill.

Saturday, 10. Partly cloudy and pleasant. At sea, enroute to Honolulu. In line all day towing Whipple. General field day.

Sunday, 11. Partly cloudy and warm. At sea, enroute to Honolulu. In line with tows. Mustered at Sunday quarters for inspection. Chaplain held divine service.

Monday, 12. Partly cloudy and warm, gentle breezes. At sea, enroute to Honolulu. In line with tows until 8.30 a.m. when changed formation to line of bearing. Stopped at 9 for California to send provisions to Truxtun, went ahead at 9.13. Sub-caliber practice. Had collision drill. Stopped at 7.49 for destroyers to haul in sub-caliber targets. Went ahead at 7.59.

Tuesday, 13. Clear and pleasant. At sea, enroute to Honolulu. NW ¼ W with tows, distance 1500 yards. California shifted position to starboard of Washington. Battery, Morris tube and sub-caliber practice. Had collision drill.

Wednesday, 14. Partly cloudy and warm to cloudy and overcast with rain. At sea, enroute to Honolulu. In line of bearing N.N.W. towing Whipple. At 11.30 a.m. cast off tows, formed column, open order, natural order distance 750 yards, destroyers on port hand. Hopkins' steering gear jammed. Whipple assisted her and they regained position at 10 p.m. Had collision drill.

Thursday, 15. Overcast and cloudy with heavy rain. Strong gale. Rough sea. At 6.10 shipped sea and carried away forward section of awning and stanchion. Bent jackstaff. Slowed down, took in awning and ventilators. Washington left formation and took Hopkins in tow. At 8.20 a.m. shipped sea and lost jackstaff and ventilator cowl. At 2 p.m. slowed down and waited for Washington. California, with Whipple and Truxtun, went ahead for Honolulu. Took position 3 points off port quarter of Washington, distance 1500 yards. Kept search lights and whistle going all night.

Friday, 16. Cloudy, overcast and rainy. Fresh to moderate gale. At sea, enroute to Honolulu. Rough sea, moderating last part. Search lights and fog whistle going until daylight. On port quarter of Washington, 1200 yards distant, making 8 knots.

Saturday, 17. Partly cloudy and squally first part, then clear and warm. Washington towing Hopkins. In position off port quarter of Washington. Sighted land at 7.50 a.m. At 8.11 a.m. went ahead full speed and took position at head of column. At 10.07 took on pilot and entered Honolulu

harbor and moored to Oceanic dock. At 10.10 French man-of-war Catinat fired salute of 13 guns, returned gun for gun. Commandant of Naval Station called officially. Division Commander and Commanding Officer called on Commander-in-Chief. Commodore Buchard, Commanding French Naval Division of Pacific Fleet, Flagship Catinat, called officially on board. Rigged coaling gear until 3.15, when started to coal, stopping at 9 p.m.

Sunday, 18. Partly cloudy, pleasant and warm; passing showers. Moored to dock, Honolulu. Coaling ship all day, finished at 6 p.m., having taken 1528 tons. Division Commander and Commanding Officer called on Commodore Buchard, on the French man-of-war Catinat. Sent patrol and liberty party ashore.

Monday, 19th. Clear and warm, with passing showers. Moored to dock at Honolulu. General field day after coaling. Washington's race boat defeated the California. Commodore Buchard called on the Commander-in-Chief. Sent liberty party ashore. Transferred short term men to Solace for transportation to United States and discharge from service.

Tuesday, 20. Partly cloudy and pleasant. Moored to dock, Honolulu. S.S. Manchuria came in from China. Race boat was defeated by the South Dakota's boat. Received stores.

Wednesday, 21. Fair and warm. Moored to dock, Honolulu. Receiving stores. Sent liberty party ashore.

Thursday, 22. Fair and pleasant. Moored to dock, Honolulu, and at sea, enroute to Magdalena Bay, Mexico. Hoisted boats and prepared for sea. At 7 a.m cast off lines, left dock and joined ships outside of harbor. Took destroyer Whipple in tow and formed column. At 8.45 the West Virginia came out and went to head of column. Took position astern of Colorado at 10.10 a.m. At 10.59 formed line of divisions, 4000 yards. At 1.10 changed to cruising formation. Had collision drill.

Friday, 23. Partly cloudy and pleasant. At sea, enroute to Magdalena Bay. In cruising formation towing Whipple. Had battle drill. Exercised gun divisions at drill.

Saturday, 24. Partly cloudy and pleasant. At sea, enroute to Magdalena Bay. In cruising formation towing Whipple. General field day. Had collision drill. Exercised at searchlight drill.

Sunday, 25. Clear and pleasant. At sea, enroute to Magdalena Bay. In cruising formation towing Whipple. Mustered at Sunday quarters for inspection. Chaplain held divine service.

It is easy enough for the forecastle guys,
The after guards to kid,
But the boy worth while,
Is the boy with the smile,
When a cinder gets under his lid.

I had a lonesome ten spot,
On a bright October day;
I put it on the raceboat—
And watched it fade away.

Changes in Rating, Etc.

September, 1908

Bowerman, R., yeo2c to yeo1c, Valliere, P. J., f2c to cp, Young, C. G., matt2c to stg ck, Thomas, W. A., chyeo (actg appt) to chyeo (per appt), Murray, J. E., gm3c to sea, Wallace, J. R., yeo3c to yeo2c, Welsch, J. L., sea to cox. The following ordinary seamen were rated seamen: Brulard, J. M., Bell, F. G., Critchfield, W. N., Hicks, C. E., Kirk, J. H., Lechlider, E. A., Neibich, H. G., Nickerson, H. N., Persing, J. E., Potter, S. P., Ritz, C, Snyder, L. A., Wright, G. E., Wenige, A., Haynes, H., Cave, G. W., Barnes, F. L., Conway, F. A., Cunneen, C. M., Perkins, H. C., Frisby, T. M., Huff, J. A., Jones, R. B., Marshburn, W. B., Williams, C. H., Williamson, G. L., Costello, J., Richter, O. W., Russell, C. I., Waller, H., Hermer, G.

October, 1908

McGrath, D., os to cp, Mitchell, W. H., cp to os, Balla, S., sea to gm3c, Walker, P. B., sea to gm3c, Crawford, B. F., sea to qm3c, Merganz, R., cox to sea, Teubert, C. J., f1c to mm2c, Kane, O, f1c to wt, Glass, A. W., f1c to wt, Yaeger, A. L., f1c to wt, Fitzpatrick, H., f1c to oil, Smith, M. F., f1c to oil, Dillon, W. F., f1c to oil, Abbot, E. J., f1c to oil, Deane, J., f1c to oil.

Ratings and Disratings--*Continued*

Bunce, E. H., cp to f2c, Brule, R. J., f2c to f1c, Nickert, E. F., cp to f2c, Cohen, G., cp to f2c, Zook, H., cp to f2c, McCabe, K. W., cp to f2c, Buder, T. A., Walker, E. B., Gibbon, R., Wilson, F. T., Zielinski, W, Johnson, J. O., Kite, H., f2c to f1c; Olsen, O. L., sea to cox, Qualey, F., gm3c to gm2c, Finnerty, N., chtc (actg appt) to chtc (per appt), Avery, J., matt3c to matt2c, McSweeney, J. P., sc3c to sc2c, Weiss, J., cp to bak2c, Young, J. A., f1c to f2c, Birx, F., f1c to f2c.

Enlisted

Oct. 21, 1908.—Landis, L. D., mm2c

Transferred

Sept., 1908.—Krause, F., bm2c, Naval Hospital, Mare Island, Cal.; Pritchard, C, os, Independence; Stein, S., f1c, Solace; McCarty, B. P., f1c, Solace; Park, E. D., cp, Annapolis.

Oct., 1908.—Wollett, R., mm2c, Truxtun; Papi, S, matt3c, Solace; Perkins, C. E., qm3c, Solace; Anderson, A., bm1c, Solace; Bennett, J. O., f1c, Solace; Balla, S., gm3c, Solace; Atkins, I. V., pvt, Solace: Kuba, F. J., f2c, Solace.

Received on Board

Sept., 1908.—Lynch, W. J., f1c, Solace; Donnelly, D., wt, Solace.

Oct., 1908.—Donegan, W. W., mm2c, Truxtun.

In the Ring

At the Independence Club, at Honolulu, before a large and enthusiastic audience, among which all ships of the fleet were represented; also, the leading sporting men of Honolulu, the Tennessee's representative, L. Frommer, master-at-arms, added another laurel to the long list of the ship by defeating J. Sherlock, welterweight champion of the Pacific Fleet (pride of the Washington), in the seventh round of their bout, which was to have been of fifteen rounds duration.

The Honolulu Evening Bulletin, in recounting the event, contained the following:

"The mill was a great one—great in every particular; it was cleanly fought, cleanly refereed, cleanly conducted, and in every way above reproach. No better go has ever been offered here.

"It was the same old story, of the old school against the new—Tom Sharkey versus Bob Fitzsimmons. Sherlock was there; he took his grueling like a Spartan, and tried to come back, but the pitiless arms of Frommer, working like automatons, kept up their activity and inch by inch the champion was beaten into insensibility. When Frommer and Sherlock took their positions at the opening of the go, it did not seem possible that the challenger could escape coming to grief. Sherlock, stocky, big of neck, and with muscles that, though pliable, stood out all over his body, looked a formidable customer for any man. Frommer, tall, thin, and rather pale-looking, seemed out-classed. But hardly had the gong sounded when the fallacy of snap judgment was shown. Frommer was evidently very much there!"

It was a good fight, won cleanly and fairly. Frommer deserves much credit for the way he handled his man, and that the decision was popular was evidenced by the loud cheering at the ringside.

Two other events were scheduled between Sam Trinkle, from the fleet, and a San Francisco lad named Smith. This was a strenuous bout, but at the end of the fifteenth was called a draw. Two colored heavyweights, Turpin, from the South Dakota, and Turner, from the California, also fought a very interesting and clever bout, the decision of which was given as a draw.

The Race Boat

Our race boat received rather a disastrous setback in an encounter with the sturdy crew from the South Dakota. A race having been arranged on the recent southern voyage, to take place after the return voyage, three days after arriving in Honolulu, on the morning of the 20th, the boats appeared on a measured three-mile straight-away course at the entrance of Honolulu harbor. Both boats seemed trained for the minute and were anxiously waiting. On the get-away, both boats did well and held together for the first mile, but after that the quick stroke of the South Dakota's crew appeared to be too much for our boys and they were not in the race after the second mile, but stuck gamely to the finish, though defeated by nearly two minutes. The South Dakota really had a slight advantage, having arrived in Honolulu four days before the Tennessee, and, as little training can be done at sea, they were no doubt in better shape than our crew.

Our crew was made up as follows: J. Manning, coxswain; H. B. Anderson, O. Kane, W. F. Dillon, T. W. Tatcher, F. Lorenzen, E. J. Abbott, E. L. Weissberg, W. N. Wright, C. A. Reddington, R. J. Bruel, J. J. Bennet, J. B. Stevens.

About $3500.00 changed hands, the last two figures coming to the Tennessee; but we know our boys did their best, and we will back them again at some future date, when we trust they will uphold the reputation of the Tennessee—"A winner in everything."

Baseball

The hotly contested and long drawn out struggle for the baseball supremacy of the Second Division of the U. S. Pacific Fleet was decisively settled at Honolulu on October 19th and 21st, the Tennesee's team defeating both the Washington and California.

The games were played on the league grounds and were extremely interesting, both to bluejacket and civilian, from start to finish.

In the first game, with the Washington, the Tennessee's pitcher seemed to have a hoodoo on the Washington team, as they were unable to place any safe ones and were defeated by the score of 2 to 0.

Then came the California's team—the team that twice had killed penant aspirations; and they played baseball all the time too, but not enough to win, the ninth inning ending with the score 4-3.

It is unnecessary to say that the Second Division teams have been very closely matched, as this is readily seen by the number of games played and the length of time necessary to develop a winner, two extra series having been required.

"The Volunteer" desires to congratulate the team of the Tennessee not only on winning a hard fought victory, but on its gentlemanly playing and conduct at all times.

No difficulty is anticipated in the battle with the best team of the First Division for the fleet championship, which will probably take place in Magdalena Bay during November.

Following is a summary of games played and the standing of the Second Division teams at the end of the series:

Oct. 19.—Tennessee 2, Washington 0. Oct. 21.—Tennessee 4, California 3.

STANDING OF SECOND DIVISION.

Tennessee	9	4	.692
Washington	7	5	.583
California	7	5	.583
South Dakota	0	9	.000

How much did you lose?

Why is our boatswain's mate like a door latch? "A cinch," said the very ordinary seaman; "Easy to rattle."

Speak up! Speak up! Angrily yelled the time-orderly to the forward bridge. Aw go on, said the signal boy; to talk through this thing you have to speak down.

ABOOKS

ALIVE Book Publishing and ALIVE Publishing Group
are imprints of Advanced Publishing LLC,
3200 A Danville Blvd., Suite 204, Alamo, California 94507

Telephone: 925.837.7303
alivebookpublishing.com